A Primer of
Transference-Focused
Psychotherapy for the Borderline Patient

A Primer of
Transference-
Focused
Psychotherapy for the
Borderline Patient

Frank E. Yeomans, John F. Clarkin,
and Otto F. Kernberg

A JASON ARONSON BOOK

ROWMAN & LITTLEFIELD PUBLISHERS, INC.
Lanham • Boulder • New York • Toronto • Oxford

A JASON ARONSON BOOK

ROWMAN & LITTLEFIELD PUBLISHERS, INC.

Published in the United States of America
by Rowman & Littlefield Publishers, Inc.
A wholly owned subsidiary of The Rowman & Littlefield Publishing Group, Inc.
4501 Forbes Boulevard, Suite 200, Lanham, Maryland 20706
www.rowmanlittlefield.com

PO Box 317
Oxford
OX2 9RU, UK

Library of Congress Cataloging-in-Publication Data

Yeomans, Frank E., 1949–
   A primer of transference-focused psychotherapy for borderline patients /
by Frank E. Yeomans, John F. Clarkin, & Otto F. Kernberg.
      p. ; cm.
   Includes bibliographical references and index.
   ISBN 0–7657–0355–6
   1. Psychotherapy.   2. Transference (Psychology)   3. Borderline
personality disorder — Treatment.   I. Clarkin, John F.
II. Kernberg, Otto F., 1928–   III. Title.
   [DNLM: 1. Borderline Personality Disorder — therapy.
2. Psychotherapy — methods.   3. Transference (Psychology).
WM 190 Y46p 2002]
RC569.5.B67 .Y457 2002

                                                      2001045978

Printed in the United States of America

∞™ The paper used in this publication meets the minimum requirements of American
National Standard for Information Sciences—Permanence of Paper for Printed Library
Materials, ANSI/NISO Z39.48-1992.

To

Clara M. Yeomans

CONTENTS

PART II:
WHAT IS THE ESSENCE OF THE TREATMENT?

PART III:
TREATMENT STRATEGIES

PART IV:
TREATMENT TACTICS

PART IV-A:
TACTIC #1—CONTRACT SETTING

PART IV-B:
CHOOSING THE PRIORITY THEME TO ADDRESS

PART IV-C:
THE REMAINING TACTICS

PART V:
TREATMENT TECHNIQUES

PART VIII:
COMMON COMPLICATIONS OF TREATMENT

PART IX:
REQUIREMENTS FOR DOING TFP

PART X:
PRACTICAL QUESTIONS
IN DELIVERING THE TREATMENT

PREFACE

Working with borderline patients is considered one of the most challenging tasks in the field of mental health. Nevertheless, persistent efforts in studying this pathology and in refining therapeutic methods have produced more effective treatment approaches. Transference-focused psychotherapy (TFP) is the most highly developed psychodynamically-based treatment for borderline personality disorder and the broader category of borderline personality organization. TFP offers an approach that respects the individual-oriented ethos of psychoanalytic work in general but that is systematized so that it can be learned and applied by therapists at different levels of training. We are grateful to our publisher, Jason Aronson, for proposing that it is time to describe this treatment in a format that will make it more accessible to students and clinicians who may have hesitated to consider an approach that is often considered esoteric and abstract in the current climate as well as to experienced psychodynamic therapists who need help treating their borderline patients. There are many others we wish to thank: our patients, for whom the struggle is the greatest and who teach us as well as learn from us; our students, especially those at the centers (White Plains, New York; Quebec; Munich; Amsterdam; Leiden, Holland; Maastricht, Holland; and Lausanne, Switzerland) who have asked the questions and presented the problems that have helped us advance our thinking; our department chairman, Dr. Jack Barchas, who has generously supported our efforts at the Personality Disorders Institute (PDI) of the Weill Cornell School of Medicine; our colleagues at the PDI who have provided a challenging and supportive academic atmosphere within which we hope to continue to generate ideas and refine treatment methods; and our secretaries, Lillian Conklin, Nina Huza, and Louise Taitt, who have provided their characteristic support and assistance.

Part I

WHO ARE THE PATIENTS? DIAGNOSTIC ISSUES

1. What is borderline personality disorder (BPD)?

BPD is a prevalent and enduring psychiatric condition. It is estimated to affect between 0.2 and 4.6% of the population.[1] The most standard current definition of BPD is that of the American Psychiatric Association's *Diagnostic and Statistical Manual, 4th Edition*.[2] Approximately 11% of psychiatric outpatients and 19% of inpatients meet these criteria.[3]

"A pervasive pattern of instability of interpersonal relationships, self-image, and affects marked by impulsivity beginning by early adulthood and present in a variety of contexts, as indicated by five (or more) of the following criteria:

1. Frantic efforts to avoid real or imagined abandonment. Note: do not include suicidal or self-mutilating behavior covered in criterion 5.
2. A pattern of unstable and intense interpersonal relationships characterized by alternating between extremes of idealization and devaluation.
3. Identity disturbance: markedly and persistently unstable self-image or sense of self.
4. Impulsivity in at least two areas that are potentially self-damaging, such as spending, sex, substance abuse, reckless driving, binge eating. Note: Do not include suicidal or self-mutilating behavior covered in criterion 5.

1. M.M. Weissman. "The epidemiology of personality disorders," in R. Michels, A.M. Cooper, S.B. Guze, L.L. Judd, A.J. Solnit, A.J. Stundard, & M.M. Weissman (Eds.), *Psychiatry*. (Philadelphia: Raven-Lippincott, 1993), Vol. 1, Chap. 15.2, pp. 1–11.

2. American Psychiatric Association. *Diagnostic and Statistical Manual of Mental Disorders, 4th edition*, (Washington, DC, 1994), p. 654.

3. Skodol, A.E., Gunderson, J.G., Livesley, W.J., Pfoli, B., Siever, L.J., Widiger, T.A. "The Borderline Diagnosis is from the Perspectives of Psychopathology, Comorbidity, Personality Structure, Biology, Genetics and Course" (2000). Manuscript submitted for publication.

5. Recurrent suicidal behavior, gestures, or threats, or self-mutilating behavior.
6. Affective instability due to a marked reactivity of mood (for example, intense episodic dysphoria, irritability, or anxiety usually lasting a few hours and only rarely more than a few days).
7. Chronic feelings of emptiness.
8. Inappropriate intense anger or difficulty controlling anger (for example, frequent displays of temper, constant anger, recurrent physical fights).
9. Transient, stress-related, paranoid ideation or severe dissociative symptoms."

This definition is primarily based on the description of symptoms and is therefore categorical in nature, although *identity disturbance* and, to some degree *affective instability* and *chronic feelings of emptiness*, involve psychological constructs that go beyond the descriptive level of the other criteria. By allowing a diagnosis of borderline personality when any five of these nine criteria are present, this definition is in accord with the fact that individuals with borderline personality form a somewhat heterogeneous group.[4] In reading this book, it is important to keep in mind that while borderline patients share a certain core pathology, they can have very different clinical presentations. Our clinical examples will convey how some patients may present as more overtly aggressive while others may present as more withdrawn and so on. In any case, the fact that this DSM-IV definition is based more on a description of symptoms than on dimensions of psychological constructs, renders it more narrow and limited than the concept of borderline personality organization.

---

4. J.F. Clarkin, P.A. Foelsch, Kin Levy, J.W. Hull, J.C. Delaney, & O.F. Kernberg. The Development of a Psychodynamic Treatment for Patients with Borderline Personality Disorder: A Preliminary Study of Behavioral Change. *Journal of Personality Disorders*, 15, (2001): 487–495.

2. What is the borderline personality organization (BPO) and how does it provide a broader understanding and conceptual framework than borderline personality disorder (BPD)?

BPO is a concept developed by Kernberg to describe a range of psychological functioning.[5] Borderline personality organization is situated between the higher level neurotic personality organization and the lower level psychotic personality organization. BPO includes both the DSM-IV borderline personality disorder and also the following DSM-IV personality disorders: schizoid, schizotypal, paranoid, histrionic, narcissistic, antisocial, and dependent. In addition, BPO includes certain personality disorders described in the psychoanalytic tradition, but not included in the DSM-IV: sadomasochistic, hypochondriasis, and the syndrome of malignant narcissism. The neurotic level of personality organization includes the obsessive-compulsive, depressive-masochistic, and hysterical personality disorders. The psychotic level of personality organization includes atypical psychoses.

For practical purposes, this system places all the severe personality disorders generally encountered in practice into the same category and links these disorders in terms of three broad areas of psychological functioning. The clinical advantage of this system is that the common features of these individual disorders lend to their effective treatment by the same model of therapy. In other words, the treatment we will describe in this book is not just for borderline personality disorder as defined in the narrow DSM-IV sense, but has a broad spectrum of utilization for all the personality disorders at the borderline level of personality organization. From a clinical point of view, an individual diagnosed with any of the specific personality disorders in the borderline range will present with: 1.) nonspecific ego weakness, 2.) disturbed interpersonal relations,

---

5. O.F. Kernberg, *Borderline Conditions and Pathological Narcissism.* (New York: Jason Aronson, 1975),

Personality Disorders: Their Mutual Relationships

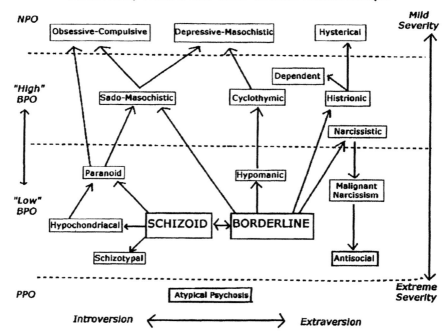

3.) difficulty with commitment to love and work, 4.) some degree of pathology in sexual relations, and 5.) superego pathology.

The determination of an individual's level of personality organization is made by assessing the following three psychological domains:

1. Identity integration versus identity diffusion;
2. Habitual level of defense mechanisms; and
3. Nature of reality testing.

The borderline level of personality organization includes those individuals with:

1. Identity diffusion;
2. Habitual use of primitive defenses; and
3. Generally intact reality testing, although reality testing can be subject to temporary breaks under stress.

3. What is identity diffusion?

Identity diffusion refers to a psychological structure characterized by the fragmentation rather than integration of the representations of the self and of others that are internalized in the course of an individual's development. Individuals with identity diffusion may feel a lack of substance or of a center. They face life without consistent beliefs, values or goals, and do not have a clear sense of direction. What is meaningful for them may be excessively determined by the context in which they find themselves. Identity diffusion will be explained in more detail (see question 8) after a review of the Object Relations Model (see question 6).

4. What is reality testing?

Normal *reality testing* involves three elements:

1. The capacity to differentiate self from non-self,
2. The capacity to differentiate intrapsychic from external origins of stimuli and perceptions, and
3. The capacity to maintain empathy with an understanding of ordinary socially conventional criteria of reality.

5. What are primitive defense mechanisms?

The concept of *primitive defense mechanisms* may need further elaboration. Defense mechanisms in general are the means by which the mind negotiates conflicts coming from the competing pressures exerted by affect states, the related drives, internalized prohibitions against drives, and the constraints of external reality. In the course of normal psychological development, individuals proceed from the primitive defenses that predominate in infancy and childhood to the mature defenses that predominate in the psychological life of the healthy individual. Mature defenses, such as rationalization, intellectualization, humor, and sublimation provide for *flexibility* in dealing with internal psychological conflicts and in adapting to the complexities of external reality.

In contrast, primitive defenses are rigid and inflexible, and do not allow for successful adaptation to external reality. They originate in the first years of life when the developing child is attempting to cope with the interface of intense affects and their related drives in relation to each other and in relation to external reality. A first effort at protecting from the anxiety of colliding libidinal and aggressive affects is to strictly separate these affects, and to separate the objects of these affects. We will explain this in more detail in the discussion of object relations theory. For now, the essential point is that primitive defenses are organized around *splitting*, the radical separation of good and bad affect, of good and bad object. These defense mechanisms protect an idealized segment of the individual's psyche, or internal world, from an aggressive segment. This separation is maintained at the expense of the integration of the images in the psyche. *Since these defenses do not lend to successful cognitive processing of the external world or of internal affects, they often lead to behavioral manifestations of distress rather than internal mastery of it.*

This split internal organization of the psyche imposes itself on the individual's perception of the world, which is experienced in categorical terms. Opinions are strong, but not stable. Things are good or bad, but what is good and what is bad can shift according to the immediate circumstances. These sudden changes contribute to the chaotic nature of the borderline individual's experience. If the individual feels a friend has disappointed him, that person may be abruptly relegated to a "black list"; then a positive experience may shift things back. The good/bad responses to the world influence the individual's moods: a single frustration may make everything seem bleak, resulting in a depressed mood. A happy surprise may shift everything temporarily to euphoria. The good/bad categories remain rigid, providing little flexibility for dealing with the complexity of the world and, in particular, of interpersonal interactions. The individual is not able to appreciate the subtle shadings of a situation or to tolerate ambiguity. This predisposes an individual to distortions in perceptions since the external reality is filtered through (made to conform to) a rigid and primitive internal structure. Thus, splitting does not provide for successful adaptation to life and can explain much of the emotional and interpersonal chaos in the lives of borderline patients.

6. What is object relations theory and how does it apply to borderline personality and transference-focused psychotherapy (TFP)?

Object relations theory is a development of Freudian psychoanalytic theory. Freud understood much psychopathology as the conflict between largely unconscious drives and internalized, partially unconscious prohibitions to these drives. Many symptoms could be understood as unconsciously determined compromises that provided some gratification to the drive and some honoring of the prohibition. Treatment involved helping the patient become conscious of the unconscious aspects of the conflict(s) between drive and prohibition in order to free the patient to deal with the conflict(s) on the conscious level rather by experiencing unconscious compromise-symptoms. A classic example of this is the hysterical conversion symptom in which a sexual impulse in conflict with an internal prohibition could lead to a paralysis with no physiological cause. The paralysis might provide some satisfaction of the sexual urge by establishing a focus on the body while also respecting the prohibition by inhibiting the full expression of the urge.

Object relations theory[6, 7, 8] emphasizes that the drives described by Freud, libido and aggression, are not experienced in the psyche in the abstract, but in relation to a specific other, an object. Therefore, the basic "building blocks" of psychic structure are units made up of the self, a drive or an affect related to a drive, and an other. These *units of self, other, and the affect* linking them are *object relations dyads*. What complicates this picture somewhat is the fact that the *self* and the *object* in the dyad are not accurate internal

6. M. Klein, *Envy and Gratitude*, (New York: Basic Books, 1957).

7. E. Jacobson, "The Self and the Object World," *The Psychoanalytic Study of the Child*, 9 (1954): 75–127.

8. O.F. Kernberg, *Internal World and External Reality: Object Relations Theory Applied* (New York:Jason Aronson, 1980), pp. 3–117.

representations of the entirety of the self or the other, but rather are representations of the self and other as they were experienced at specific moments in time in the course of early development. Therefore, a more precise description of the object relations dyad is a particular *representation of the self* connected by an *affect* to a particular *representation of the object*.

Theory

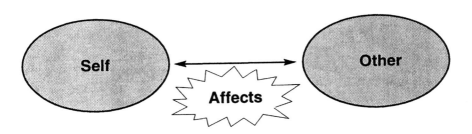

In the course of infant development, multiple internal dyads are created based on prototypical experiences.

As an infant develops, the nature of its moment-to-moment experience differs in terms of the affective intensity of the experience. During relatively quiescent periods of low affective intensity, the infant takes in the surrounding environment with a general sort of cognitive learning. This type of learning does not have a major impact on the infant's motivational system. In contrast, the infant also has periods of high affective intensity. These are usually related to experiences of a need or a wish for pleasure ("I need help/I want more") or to experiences of fear or a wish to get away from pain ("Get me away from that!"). A typical experience of pleasure/satisfaction occurs when the infant is hungry and the mother is present and responds, while a typical experience of

Patient's Inner World

S = Self-Representation
O = Object - Representation
a = Affect

Examples

S1 = Meek, abused figure
O1 = Harsh, abusing authority figure
a 1 = Fear

S2 = Childish-dependent figure
O2 = Ideal, giving figure
a2 = Love

S3 = Powerful, controlling figure
O3 = Weak, Slave-like figure
a3 = Wrath

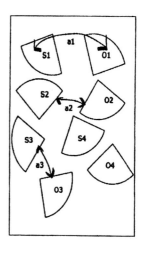

pain/frustration occurs when the mother, for whatever reason, does not respond.

These periods of peak affective intensity involve the self in relation to an other and are involved in the *laying down of affect-laden memory structures* in the developing psyche. As stated by Kernberg: "Peak-affect experiences may facilitate the internalization of primitive object relations organized along the axis of rewarding, or all-good, or aversive, or all-bad, ones. In other words, the experience of self and object when the infant is in a peak affect state acquires an intensity that facilitates the laying down of affective memory structures."[9]. These affect-laden memory structures influence the developing individual's motivational system since under peak affect states an infant is likely to memorize what seems important for survival, to obtain what is needed, and to avoid what is painful or threatening.

With regard to the object relations dyads, the infant's satisfying experiences involve an ideal image of a perfect nurturing other and a satisfied self, while the frustrating experiences involve a totally negative image of a depriving or even abusive other and a needy, helpless self. Although these images are representative of a moment in time, rather than of the totality or continuity of the object, they are encoded in memory structures as mentioned above. This system is such that an infant whose caregiver is generally attentive and nurturing may nevertheless internalize images of a sadistic, depriving object because of experiences of temporary frustration or deprivation. In a similar fashion, an infant whose caregiver is generally neglectful or abusive may have rare satisfying experiences that lead to an internalized image of a loving, nurturing object.

The infant's affects are intense since affects have the biological function of helping mammals who are immature to survive through pleasure/nurturance seeking and harm avoidance. This

---

9. O.F. Kernberg, *Aggression in Personality Disorders and Perversions* (New Haven:Yale University Press, 1992), p. 13.

intensity of affects can, of course, be the quality of affects in borderline patients. In the course of the infant's development, multiple affectively charged experiences are internalized in such a way that a segment of the psyche is built up with these idealized images based on satisfying experiences on one side, and a segment is built up with negative, aversive, devalued images on the other. An active separation of these segments develops within the psyche.

The purpose of this separation is to protect the idealized representations, imbued with warm, loving feelings toward the object perceived as satisfying, from the negative representations, associated with the affects of rage and hatred. One aspect of object relations theory that separates it from a more purely cognitive psychology is the emphasis that these representations are not merely cognitive images, but are connected to extremely intense primitive affects, especially hatred of the depriving object. Since hatred is defined by the wish to destroy, a separation of the good and bad segments is necessary in this primitive psychic organization to protect the "good" representations of self and other from the danger of destruction by the hatred associated with the "bad" ones. *This separation is the internal mechanism of splitting,* mentioned earlier as the paradigm of primitive defense mechanisms and as central to borderline pathology.

We will discuss the further development of an individual's internal world, as understood by object relations theory, in questions 8 and 13.

Split Organization

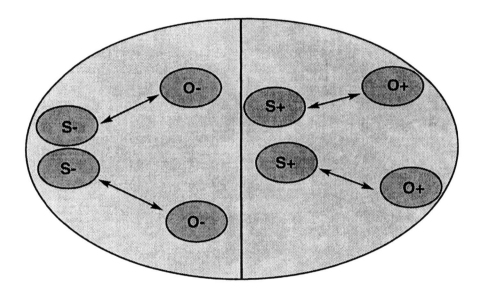

7. How are defense mechanisms understood in terms of internalized object relations?

As stated above, the concept of defense mechanisms refers to the habitual psychological strategies employed by an individual to ward off anxiety. Anxiety, from a psychoanalytic point of view, can come from internal affects, internal prohibitions, external threats, or from the conflicts between or among any of these. Defense mechanisms can be more or less mature depending on how well they help the individual adapt to life and the world around them. Generally, the use of more mature defense mechanisms comes with normal psychological development. However, some areas of psychopathology, including borderline personality, can be understood as the continued *use of primitive defense mechanisms as the primary defense mechanisms* in the adult. While it may seem odd that certain individuals would maintain this crude system, it should be remembered that even primitive defense mechanisms provide a rudimentary way of dealing with the problem of anxiety.

From the point of view of the object relations model, *the organization of self- and object-representations is intimately involved with the level of defense mechanisms*. For example, if the self- and object-representations are organized around a *fundamental split*, this split provides some form of *coping mechanism* with which to deal with the anxiety of a perceived threat—whether that threat be provoked by internal pressures or external stimuli (a distinction which is not always clear to the patient). In other words, if the primitively-organized individual is confronted with something displeasing or threatening, that object is placed in the "all-bad" category, where it is "safely" separated from anything with a good connotation.

While this is one way of trying to contain anxiety, it is at the expense of successful adaptation. For instance, if the displeasing feeling comes from within the self, the self may then become the object of hatred and attack. Alternatively, the displeasing feeling in the self may be denied as part of the self and experienced as coming from outside, leading to confusion and, consequently, poor adaptation to reality. Hence, splitting is often manifested as a primitive form of *projection* when one part of the split is experienced as originating in an external object.

Other primitive defense mechanisms stem from the split internal organization:

— *projective identification* is characterized by an *unconscious tendency to both induce in an other what is being projected and to attempt to control the other person* who is assumed to function under the dominance of the projected aspect of the patient. As compared to simple projection, projective identification involves ways in which the patient can induce in the other, such as the therapist, a disavowed part of the self. For example, patients who cannot tolerate their feelings of aggression may provoke and frustrate the therapist in subtle (and sometimes not so subtle) ways that lead to the therapist experiencing the affect (aggression) disavowed by the patient. The affect is less threatening/disturbing to the patient if it is perceived as coming from outside and if, unconsciously, the patient has a sense of controlling it.

The nature of projective identification is one of the reasons therapists must be very attuned to their countertransference. Therapists' awareness that certain of their own feelings may reflect denied aspects of the patient's internal world helps the therapist acquire the data necessary to understand that internal world.

— *primitive idealization/devaluation* is the manifestation of the classic "all-good/all-bad" split. This can take different forms in therapy. Sometimes the therapist is devalued in comparison to someone else or to the patient who is idealized. For example, the patient may say:

> *You know nothing about taking care of people. The minister in my church back home really knew how. If only he were here instead of you . . . ,* or *I'm supposed to be the sick one, but I'm a paragon of health compared to you. At least I know something about compassion.*

I care about people. I have values. You sit there doing nothing, making a huge income off of poor people who are stupid enough to come to see you. You're evil.

Alternately, patients may idealize the therapist and devalue themselves:

I'm hopeless. Here I am, twenty-five years old, and I don't even have a college degree. You're so smart and educated. Even if I got better, I could never be happy because I couldn't be like you and the people you associate with [which, of course, is what the patient imagines].

— *denial* in borderline patients is generally in the form of denial of the impact of experiencing two emotionally independent areas of consciousness, the two sides of the internal split. Patients may be aware that their perceptions, thoughts, and feelings may be completely opposite from one time to another but this awareness has no emotional impact and does not influence their feelings in the present moment. The patient demonstrates a marked lack of concern or anxiety about contradictions of which he is cognitively aware. This can be evidenced as indifference about situations involving risk to his own well-being or to important relationships. An example is a patient who reported with no sign of concern that he had a habit of driving around an extremely dangerous part of the city by himself late at night.

This discussion of denial highlights *the important fact that borderline individuals experience some degree of awareness of both sides of their internal conflict although this awareness is not combined into an integrated whole.* At one point in time they experience the positive side of the split with a varying mix of preoedipal wishes for nurturing and of oedipal eroticism (more mature, but conflicted, sexual desire). At another point they experience the negative side of the split with the hateful wish for destruction. The art of therapy with borderline patients is to understand the obstacles to integrating these co-existent sides into a more nuanced whole.

In contrast, the neurotic individuals are characterized by conflicts where repression is the key factor. Repression is a more stable state of internal separation of more highly organized competing intrapsychic forces than are present in splitting. In neurotic individuals, the unconscious material (usually "unacceptable" impulses) is consistently repressed and comes to conscious awareness only with slow, laborious work in therapy. In contrast, borderline individuals have alternating awareness of the different sides of their internal conflict, but *denial* allows them to tolerate this state of affairs without the anxiety that would be associated with co-consciousness of contradictory material.

— *omnipotence and omnipotent control*[10] are a response to the chronic underlying paranoid transference typical of most borderline patients at the beginning of therapy (see evolution of chronic transferences in Part II, question 17). This baseline paranoid transference involves a fundamental distrust of others, a belief that allowing oneself to give in to the longing for closeness with an other would inevitably result in rejection, abandonment, exploitation, humiliation, or abuse. Consequently, patients may feel safe only if they feel in control of the object they are relating to. In sessions, this can be seen most dramatically in the apparently paradoxical situation of a patient, who comes to therapy seeking help, monopolizing the sessions by talking non-stop, and not allowing the therapist to intervene. Whenever the therapist does manage to interject a comment, the patient tends to ignore or dismiss it summarily. This makes sense from the point of view of someone who goes through life with the (often unconscious) conviction that eventually any other will leave or mistreat them. It follows that a paramount consideration would then be to control the other as best one can, often in a way that does not allow the other to enter into the patient's life meaningfully, that drains the other of any depth or individuality and that leaves the patient with

---

10. O.F. Kernberg, "Omnipotence in the Transference and in the Countertransference," *The Scandinavian Psychoanalytic Review* 18(1995):2–21.

a hollow sense of his own importance in relation to this "cardboard figure" he creates of the therapist. Ironically, it is often precisely the unempathic, arrogant, monopolizing, devaluing, and rejecting behavior that makes up omnipotent control that drives others away.

8. How does the development of internal psychological structure differ in normal individuals as compared to individuals with borderline personality?

In normal development, integration of the split-off good and bad segments takes place between the ages of one and three, leading to an internal world no longer characterized by this split, but rather by representations of self and other which include both good and bad characteristics, allowing for a flexibility in the personality which is more adaptable to the complexities of the real world.

In effecting this integration, the individual moves from the realm of ideal, perfect providers and sadistic persecutors to that of the "good enough" other, a more realistic position. This integration of internal images is driven by two factors. The first is cognitive development—that is, most individuals' ability to perceive that the split model of extreme opposites does not fit the complexity of real people. The second factor is the prevalence of good, satisfying experiences over bad, frustrating ones in the personal develop-ment of most individuals; this prevalence of good experiences helps tolerate some bad without the extreme reaction of hatred. This development of integration corresponds to the *depressive position* described by Melanie Klein. While depressive position may sound like an undesirable state of affairs, it is preferable to the *paranoid schizoid position* which precedes it and which is character-ized by the unrealistically extreme internal representations de-scribed above. This position is called paranoid because the bad, persecutory side of the split is generally projected onto external objects leaving the individual in a habitual expectation of aggres-sion from the outside. The depressive position is labeled as such both because it entails the loss of the image of the ideal provider, thus involving mourning of this ideal object, and because it involves experiencing guilt for the hatred that had been directed toward the "bad object" which is now accepted as part of a more complex integrated object.

Normal Organization

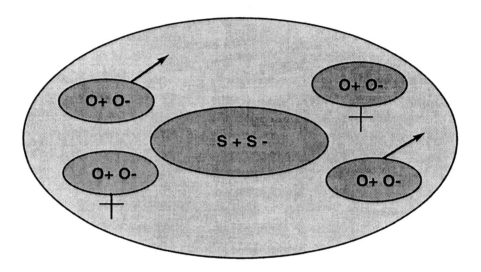

If the psychological integration that leads to the depressive position does not take place, the individual is left with the split internal organization that, in later life, corresponds to borderline personality. *Identity diffusion* stems from the fragmented nature of this split internal organization. Multiple unintegrated self-object dyads variously determine the individual's subjective experience at any given moment, creating a sense of discontinuity of experience and great difficulty in committing to relationships, meaningful work, goals, or values.

9. What is psychic structure?

This state of "internal split versus integration" is at the core of what we refer to as psychic structure. In the course of normal development, psychic structure is elaborated as the object relations dyads re-group to form Freud's tripartite structure of the id, superego, and ego.[11] However, individuals with borderline personality organization do not resolve the split structure sufficiently to achieve the more fully developed tripartite structure described by Freud. For the purposes of this primer, we will keep the discussion of psychic structure at the very basic level of a split versus an integrated structure, since the goal of TFP is to help the patient advance from the former to the latter.

---

11. O.F. Kernberg, Freud conserved and revised: an interview with David Scharff. In: *The psychoanalytic century: Freud's Legacy for the Future.* Edited by D. Scharff. (New York: Other Press, 2001.)

10. Are there circumstances in which adults who are not borderline function at a split level of psychic organization?

Yes. One example is the experience of infatuation when falling in love; this includes an element of regression to a state of experiencing the other as "all-good." One can also find a primitive level of psychological functioning in couples whose long-term intimate relationships may involve a mutual projective identification, each inducing in the other affects they do not acknowledge in themselves.[12]

Another example is that of large, unstructured group processes. The anxiety an individual experiences in such situations leaves that person prone to seeing any threat or menace as "all-bad." This regression in group settings can explain why otherwise mature individuals are capable of extreme and irrational actions as part of an unstructured group.[13]

---

12. H.V. Dicks, *Marital Tensions* (London: Karnac Books, Basic Books, 1967), pp. 70–84.

13. W.R. Bion, *Experiences in groups and other papers* (New York: Basic Books, 1961), pp. 141–143.

11. In the primitively organized split psyche, what interactions might be expected within and among the object relations dyads?

While each dyad, in the unintegrated state of the psyche, may have a rigid and fixed quality to it, the dyads can shift in a number of ways. First, one dyad may abruptly replace another as the one that is currently active in determining the individual's subjective experience at a given moment.

Second, the poles of a dyad may abruptly shift in the sense that the characteristics of the object may suddenly become those of the self, and vice versa. This shift is represented in the top two lines of Figure 6.

It is especially interesting that these shifts, while they have a large influence on the individual's subjective experience and actions, often take place outside an individual's awareness. For example, a patient who experiences himself as the victim in a situation may abruptly take on the role of abuser by becoming angry and aggressive without being consciously aware of the change in role. The patient may be aware that his behavior has changed but with no awareness that this behavior represents an identification with an aggressive figure; instead, his subjective experience may be that the behavior is rather the justified response/reaction of an abused figure and a continuation of that role.

A third way the dyads may interact is that one dyad may exist in a tense opposition to the opposite dyad, as represented in the relation between the first and third lines in Figure 6. For example, a dyad involving a suspicious and fearful self in relation to a persecutory object may exist in opposition to a dyad involving a self that longs for nurturing in relation to a perfectly nurturing object. The dyad that is predominant at a given point in time defends against awareness of the opposing dyad. The instability of the system is such that what is at one time the defended-against dyad may become the predominant dyad and vice versa. This concept will be illustrated in clinical examples to follow.

Patient's Inner World

S = Self-Representation
O = Object - Representation
a = Affect

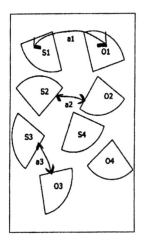

Examples

S1 = Meek, abused figure
O1 = Harsh, abusing authority figure
a 1 = Fear

S2 = Childish-dependent figure
O2 = Ideal, giving figure
a2 = Love

S3 = Powerful, controlling figure
O3 = Weak, Slave-like figure
a3 = Wrath

OBJECT RELATIONSHIP INTERACTIONS:
OSCILLATION AND DEFENSE

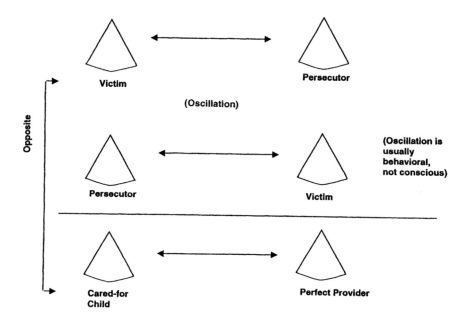

12. How does one assess for BPO and BPD?

The *structural interview*[14] is a clinical assessment that both provides an organized method to systematic assessment and also encourages the use of insight and intuition in using the interaction with the patient to guide the evaluation. Briefly, this interview involves taking a thorough inventory of the patient's symptoms and inquiring about the patient's attitude toward and understanding of them. After this survey of symptoms, the patient's conception of self and self in relation to important others is examined, along with historical information about relations with others. Only after this survey of symptoms and review of relations is a traditional personal developmental history elicited.

As the term structural interview implies, the interview puts more emphasis on assessing the current psychic structure (see questions 8 and 9 above) than on personal history. During the course of the interview, the therapist is careful to assess the level of the patient's defenses, the quality of the patient's interpersonal relations, and the patient's capacity for reality testing.

The flow of the *structural interview* is as follows:

In the *initial phase*, the therapist starts by asking about current symptoms and the patient's attitude toward them:

> I am interested in hearing about what brought you here, what the nature of your problems or difficulties are, what you expect from treatment, and where you are now in this regard.

The therapist then inquires about the patient's view of him or herself:

> You have told me about your symptoms (or difficulties). Could you now describe yourself, your personality, what you think is important for me to get a real feeling for you as a person?

---

14. O.F. Kernberg (1981). "Structural Interviewing," *Psychiatric Clinics of North America* 4(1981):169–195.

In the *middle phase*, the therapist further pursues the patient's description of self to elicit as full a description as possible and also goes on to inquire about the patient's capacity to describe others:

> I would now like to learn more about yourself as a person, the way you perceive yourself, the way you feel other people perceive you, whatever you think might be helpful for me to gain an in-depth vision of you within the time we have.

After the patient has completed his self-description, the therapist continues:

> I would now like to ask you to tell me something about the people who are most important in your present life. Could you tell me something about them in such a way that, again, given our limited time, I might form a real, live impression of them?

The interview emphasizes the patient's descriptions of self and others in order to obtain a sense of the patient's state of identity integration versus identity diffusion. More complex but yet coherent descriptions reflect a higher the level of identity integration. More fragmented, discontinuous, contradictory or simply sparse, superficial descriptions reflect identity diffusion.

In the *advanced phase* of the interview, the therapist assesses the patient's reality testing. This is done by referring back to any elements of the patient's interview which seemed odd or contradictory and asking:

> Some things you reported to me seem to be strange, can you see what I mean by that?

The therapist ends the interview by asking:

> What do you think I should have asked you and have not asked?

13. What are the origins of borderline personality organization?

Since the principal feature of BPO is a split internal structure, one can address the question of the origins of BPO by considering what makes it difficult to move from this split structure to a more integrated structure. Discussion of etiology involves consideration of the five following interrelated factors:

1. Affects
2. Temperament
3. Character
4. Personality
5. Trauma

Affects are psychophysiological behavior patterns that include a subjective experience of a pleasurable or painful nature, a cognitive appraisal of the immediate situation, a muscular and neurovegetative discharge pattern, and, very importantly, a specific facial expression that carries a crucial communication function in the infant/caregiver interaction. Affects are strongly influenced by an individual's neurochemical system, with neurotransmitters playing an important role, potentially determining a dysfunctional intensity of affective response.

Temperament is the expression of the genetically-determined intensity, rhythm, and threshold of affect regulation. It can be considered the inborn disposition to affect regulation that determines affect activation. Temperament also includes an element of cognitive style insofar as introversion and extraversion are probably temperamental dimensions linked to affect regulation.

Character results from the interaction between temperament and the human environment. It is the integration of the habitual behavioral patterns linking temperament with object relations. In other words, character is temperament as it is expressed in the individual's habitual relations to self and others.

Personality is the integration of temperament, character, cognitive potential and internalized values. This latter concept is related to the development of the superego and is beyond the scope of the current discussion.[15]

Trauma may involve physical or sexual abuse, chronic neglect, or psychological trauma. It could also include a severely frustrating life situation, chronically painful physical illness, or early prolonged separation.

Taking into account the above factors, the most important single etiological force in the development of BPO is an excess of aggression that the individual cannot successfully integrate into one's psychological life. Rather than integrate this aggression, the individual handles it by keeping it split-off. This intense load of aggression may involve the neurochemical system of the affects, the inborn threshold of affect activation (temperament), or the interaction of character and trauma. With regard to the latter, if a child is exposed to physical or sexual abuse or neglect, there will be an increase in the internalization of object relations dyads imbued with intense negative affect. This makes the developmental task of integration of the internal world more difficult.

Under normal expectable circumstances, the developing child eventually gains the cognitive awareness that the ideal mother and the persecutory or neglectful mother are the same. Similarly, the child realizes that the lovable self and the enraged, threatened self are the same. This awareness is helped by the fact that in normal development, there is a predominance of good experiences over bad ones. This strengthens the good side of the internal world so that the child can dare to let some of the affects associated with the bad side enter the realm of the good without fearing that they will totally destroy the good. If the child has had a predominance of negative experiences, then the split-off bad side feels more powerful and threatening. Therefore, maintaining the split may seem

---

15. O.F. Kernberg (1984). *Severe Personality Disorders* (New Haven: Yale University Press, 1984), p. 277.

the only option to protect an idealized segment of psychic experience from the destructive power of the persecutory bad side with its related rage and hatred.

It is further hypothesized that the split structure is maintained over time and through repeated interactions that seem to "confirm" the validity of the established internal representations to the individual. This "confirmation" of the individual's internal world is specious and somewhat circular. It is based on two phenomena: 1) the individual's perception and experience of current interactions is not objective but is processed through a repertoire of extreme, unintegrated internal representations, leading the individual to perceive things not as they are, but rather as they are expected to be, and 2) the individual tends to act automatically in accordance with internal representations, often provoking the very reaction from others (for example, rejection or abandonment) which is both feared and expected within the individual's internal system.

From this discussion it is clear that the object relations understanding of borderline personality provides a formulation based on a deep personality structure—an internal organization of the mind that determines the individual's experience of self and others. It provides a more comprehensive understanding of the disorder than a model, or treatment, which focuses on symptoms or behaviors.

Part II

WHAT IS THE ESSENCE OF THE TREATMENT?

14. What is TFP?

Transference-focused psychotherapy, or TFP, is a specialized version of psychodynamic psychotherapy. It is based on the principles of psychodynamic psychotherapy, but includes both a special emphasis on certain aspects of psychoanalytic theory and modifications of some techniques of psychodynamic therapy in order to adequately address the special problems of borderline patients. TFP defined is defined by:

1.) Its roots in the object relations model and the ensuing emphasis on the transference as the key to understanding and change, since it is believed that the patient's internal world of object representations unfolds and is "lived" in the transference, and

2.) Its strategies, tactics, and techniques, which will be discussed in depth in later chapters. While these strategies, tactics, and techniques are somewhat complex, two essential guidelines are at the heart of TFP:

a) The therapist must attend to the establishment and maintenance of an adequate frame of treatment before any interpretive work can be done. This attention to the frame is a major task in itself, requiring skills the therapist must develop, starting with knowing how to set up an appropriate treatment contract. Without a frame in place, the chaos of borderline pathology can overwhelm the treatment.

b) Once working within the frame, the therapist must focus on the patient's internal world of relationship patterns as they unfold in the relationship with the therapist.

It can be difficult to maintain this focus for three reasons:

First, patients often discuss material from outside the sessions. While this material may be relevant if it is invested with affect (see Part IV-B, question 39 on the "economic principle"), it often serves as a distraction from what is happening in the immediate relationship in the therapy. It is important to focus on the immediate

Patient's Inner World   **Therapist as seen by Patient**

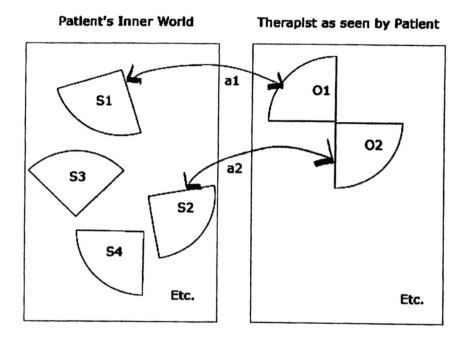

relationship because it is where the therapist can get the most accurate sense of the patient's perception of a relationship and it is where the affect is immediately present;

Second, the therapist may subtly resist addressing important aspects of the patient's internal world when the therapist senses that this might arouse an angry, defensive response from a patient;

Third, acting out may threaten the work of understanding— which is why maintaining the frame of treatment is the first order of business before exploring and interpreting the patient's internal world can be carried out.

15. What are the patient inclusion and exclusion criteria for TFP?

TFP is designed for treatment of patients with borderline personality organization (BPO). As the diagram presented earlier (Part I, question 2) indicates, BPO corresponds roughly to the so-called cluster B and C personality disorders on DSM-IV Axis II. It includes the BPD, antisocial, narcissistic personality disorders of cluster B, and the schizoid and schizotypal personality disorders of cluster C. Therefore, the major inclusion criterion is that the patient manifests borderline personality organization. It is also necessary that patients be of average intelligence or above to benefit from TFP.

The principle exclusion criteria are:

— Active substance abuse,
— Active eating disorder,
— Antisocial personality disorder,
— Secondary gain as the motivation for treatment.

To elaborate, our experience is that BPO patients with an *active* substance abuse or eating disorder need to focus on achieving control of those symptoms before they can progress to TFP. Experience has shown that six months of sobriety is an indication that substance abuse is under adequate control to start TFP. We exclude patients with true antisocial personality disorder because clinical experience shows that they do not respond to TFP or any other treatment. It is important to point out the antisocial personality disorder on DSM-IV Axis II and true psychopathic personality as understood in the Cleckley tradition are overlapping but not the same thing.[1] The DSM definition focuses on behaviors, while the full antisocial personality in the traditional sense is based on an individual's total lack of conscience and of the capacity for

---

1. H. Cleckley, *The Mask of Sanity* (4th ed.) (St. Louis: Mosby), 1976.

empathy. Such individuals have no concern for others except to the extent that they can use and exploit them as the means to an end. In contrast, an individual may meet criteria for the DSM diagnosis of antisocial personality disorder but still have some capacity for empathy and concern for another person. We would consider such individuals, who may have a history of lying, stealing, irresponsibility, and exploiting the system as having antisocial *traits*. These individuals fall within the limits of treatability, although they are the most difficult to successfully treat.

Individuals with antisocial personality can be divided into passive and aggressive types (Henderson, 1939).[2] For both of these types, the world is composed of only two sorts of people: the strong who exploit and whom they admire and fear, and the weak, who may be good and kind, but who exist to be exploited. The passive antisocial has learned to deal with the strong by feigning submission while attempting to outsmart them. Individuals with this more parasitic form of antisocial personality are like "wolves in sheep's clothing" who, in some cases, are in denial of their own aggression and justify their exploitation of others as making up for wrongs they have endured. They have at least some capacity to control immediate anger and aggression and to exercise an orchestrated exploitation. This implies a level of ego function that may allow for therapeutic intervention even though the prognosis remains very poor.

A corollary to excluding patients with antisocial personality disorder is excluding patients (who may be of the passive antisocial type) whose motivation for treatment is primarily to obtain explicit secondary gain (see Part IV-A, question 37), such as escaping from real-life responsibilities (e.g., the need to earn a living), or trying to avoid legal difficulties by taking shelter in psychotherapy.

---

2. D.K. Henderson, *Psychopathic States* (London: Chapman and Hall, 1939).

16. Aside from the strict exclusion criteria, are there other prognostic factors?

Yes, the most important prognostic factors are:

— Negative therapeutic reactions,
— The pervasiveness of aggression,
— The quality of interpersonal relationships,
— Pysical attractiveness
— Intelligence

Negative therapeutic reactions are negative responses some patients have to therapy just when there is some indication of improvement or progress. These responses appear to be paradoxical but are rooted in a patient's dynamics. There are three basic types, listed here in order of severity, from least to most severe:

1.) A negative response due to a patient's unconscious guilt about improving,

2.) A negative response due to the patient's envy of the therapist. This is typical of many narcissistic patients and, in particular, of patients with the syndrome of *malignant narcissism*. This syndrome describes the most severe level of BPO that can generally be treated (though often with difficulty). It involves a narcissistic personality with antisocial *behavior* but at least some capacity for empathy, egosyntonic aggression, and strong paranoid traits. Patients with this diagnosis experience particularly intense envy of anyone they perceive as superior to them. This can lead to a specific complication in their treatment. Just at the point when they feel the therapist is helping them, they may viciously attack the treatment or attack themselves as a way of attacking the treatment. This is because they experience the therapist's ability to help them as a sign of the therapist's superiority and consequently as a humiliation. Therefore, they may attempt to defeat their therapist, even at the expense of their physical integrity or their life, rather than allow any improvement they perceive as evidence of the therapist's superiority. If a patient presents with this dynamic, the therapist must interpret it vigorously to try to avoid the patient's "triumph in defeat."

3.) A negative response in patients who experience self-destructiveness as triumph and power over others, over pain and illness, and even over life and death. Patients with this form of reaction fall into the diagnostic categories of malignant narcissism or antisocial personality disorder. This connects with the related negative prognostic factor of the *pervasiveness of aggression*—a condition where aggression is present consistently in all domains of the patient's life.

Regarding the *quality of interpersonal relations*, it may seem self-evident that better interpersonal relations are associated with better outcome. A history of poor interpersonal relations, characterized by a lack of capacity for any depth or intimacy in relations, is a poor prognostic factor for treatment. However, it is important to note that clinical experience and research[3] have shown that even a pathological pattern of relating, such as sexual promiscuity, is a better prognostic sign than social isolation and absence of sexual relations. *Physical attractiveness* is associated with better outcome,[4] although it does not guarantee good outcome, especially in cases involving a history of incest.

---

3. J.W. Hull, J.F. Clarkin, & F.Y. Yeomans, "Borderline Personality Disorder and Impulsive Sexual Behavior," *Hospital and Community Psychiatry* 4(1993):1000–1002.

4. M. Stone, *The Fate of Borderline Patients* (New York: Guilford Press, 1990), 146–149.

17. What kind of change can be expected from TFP?

Like most treatments for BPD, TFP is a long-term treatment.[5] Unlike more behaviorally-oriented treatments, TFP aims at changing underlying personality structure as well as changing behaviors. If treatment succeeds in integrating patients' split and fragmented internal structures, patients' can experience not only symptom changes, such as a decrease in acting out behaviors, but also fundamental changes in the way they experience themselves and relationships with others, leading to a more rewarding and satisfying life experience.

In TFP, the first change observed is usually a decrease in the patient's impulsive behaviors. This is usually followed by improvement in the regulation of affects. However, the counterpoint to the improvement in the patient's behaviors outside therapy is a concentration of intense feelings within the therapy sessions. In fact, if there is not an intensification of affect in the sessions, the therapist should be concerned that the therapy is not evolving in a productive direction. A decrease in identity diffusion is generally the last and deepest change, since it comes with the integration of internal psychic structure. Clinical experience has shown that control of the most serious acting out behaviors is often achieved in the first six to twelve months of treatment. Evidence of some structural personality change (integration) has been seen after one year of treatment. However, significant structural change usually requires a minimum of two years and often many more years of treatment.

Over the course of therapy, there is usually an evolution in the patient's chronic, baseline transference. Although we have emphasized the rapid shifts that occur in the immediate transference on a moment-to-moment basis, most patients have a predominant transference that prevails over the others in determining their

---

5. J.C. Perry, E. Banon, & F. Ianni, "Effectiveness of Psychotherapy for Personality Disorders," *American Journal of Psychiatry* 156(1999):1312–1321.

experience of themselves and of the world. Most borderline patients begin therapy with a chronic paranoid transference—that is, the assumption that their desires, their preoedipal and oedipal wishes, will be met with rejection, teasing or violence. In other words, in their split internal world, an object relation from the negative side of the internal split seems more real, or safer, than an object relation from the positive side.

In the course of therapy, this chronic paranoid transference usually evolves into a depressive transference. This transference corresponds to a more integrated internal world in which 1.) the object is experienced as loving and caring—but not perfectly (the loss of the ideal object), and 2.) the self can experience love for the object that can coexist with feelings of frustration, anger, and guilt related to past destructive urges (the depressive position).

The reader is referred to Part X, question 79 for more specific data on change that was documented in an empirical investigation of the first year of treatment with TFP.

18. How does TFP modify traditional psychodynamic psychotherapy to create a treatment specific to borderline patients?

Certain modifications of traditional psychodynamic psychotherapy are required in order to apply it successfully to borderline pathology. The principle modifications are:

— TFP puts a stronger emphasis of the treatment contract
— The TFP therapist relies more on the nonverbal and countertransference channels of communication (as opposed to direct verbal communication) than in traditional therapy (see Part IV-B, question 40 for more on the channels of communication).
— The TFP therapist is generally more *active* in intervening than in traditional therapy
— TFP may require more deviation from technical neutrality
— In TFP the therapist must experience, absorb, and deal with levels of affect that are often more intense than those encountered in traditional therapy with healthier patients.

We will elaborate on these modifications in the course of the primer. For the moment, we will explain the last of these in some greater detail. Working with borderline patients requires the therapist's ability and willingness to deal with extremely strong affects. One could say that entering into the internal world of these patients involves contact with primitive material that calls for a certain emotional stamina on the part of the therapist. The unique role of the therapist is to invite these affects to emerge in a controlled environment. While the treatment environment may be controlled (through the treatment frame established by the treatment contract), the affects are nevertheless extremely intense. The therapist must be able to be exposed to and work with extremes of love and longing and hatred and aggression. In this sense, therapy is not merely an intellectual experience, although it requires both intelligence and knowledge, but also an emotional experience that requires exposure to, without involvement in, the intense affective world of the patient. A somewhat dramatic metaphor is to compare the therapist to Ulysses who, in order to hear the sirens' call without acting in response to it, had himself tied to the mast of the ship so that he could be exposed to it without responding in turn.

One particular emotional demand of the therapist is the ability to consider that a patient could, in fact, commit suicide. If therapists cannot emotionally accept this possibility, they will have great difficulty treating this patient population—the fear of suicide is likely to paralyze them from effectively doing their work. Good treatment greatly diminishes the risk of suicide, but cannot guarantee against it.

19. What are the principle alternative treatments for BPD and BPO?

We can distinguish between the *setting* of treatment, the *format* of treatment, and the *strategies and techniques* of treatment. We will first discuss setting. In their most suicidal periods, borderline patients are sometimes hospitalized to control the self-destruction.[6] Day hospital treatment is sometimes used, either following hospitalization or to avoid hospitalization, for maintenance of control and the goal of increasing daily functioning (self-scheduling, self-care, and work).[7, 8] However, outpatient care is usually the standard treatment setting for borderline patients.

The common treatment *formats* are individual, group, marital, and family treatment. Group therapy can be used in all treatment settings, and is common in inpatient and day hospital settings. Outpatient group treatment has been investigated,[9] and group skills training is an integral part of Linehan's dialectical behavior treatment.[10]

The most common treatment *strategies and techniques* that have been described for borderline patients are those of supportive treatment, cognitive-behavioral treatment, and psychodynamic treatment. Rockland has described a psychodynamically informed

6. G.O. Gabbard, L. Coyne, & J.G. Allen, "Evaluation of Intensive Inpatient Treatment of Patients with Severe Personality Disorders," *Psychiatric Services* 51(2000):893–898.

7. A. Bateman, & P. Fonagy, "The Effectiveness of Partial Hospitalization in the Treatment of Borderline Personality Disorder: A Randomized Controlled Trial," *American Journal of Psychiatry* 156(1999):1563–1569.

8. A. Bateman, & P. Fonagy, "Treatment of Borderline Personality Disorder with Psychoanalytically Oriented Partial Hospitalization: An 18-month Follow-up, *American Journal of Psychiatry* 158(2001):36–42.

9. H. Monroe-Blum, E.E. Marziali, "A Controlled Study of Short-Term Group Treatment of Borderline Personality Disorder," *Journal of Personality Disorders* 9 (1995): 190–198.

10. M.M. Linehan, *Cognitive-Behavioral Treatment for Borderline Personality Disorder* (New York: Guilford Press, 1993).

supportive treatment specifically for borderline patients.[11] This is a very carefully thought out treatment that combines consistency with support and a hopeful attitude that many therapists find appealing in their work with these patients. The goal of the treatment is to contain and sustain the patient through crisis periods, and encourage small gains over time.

The goal of Linehan's[12] cognitive-behavioral treatment is to validate the patient's perceptions and experience, and in that context to assist the patient in learning adaptive life skills especially for interpersonal contexts. The course of treatment combines individual work and group format.

There are a number of approaches to the psychodynamic treatment of borderline patients. Waldinger[13] discusses the similarities and differences among the principal psychodynamic approaches. Gunderson[14] discusses psychoanalytic contributions to individual therapy with borderlines. Most alternative psychodynamic approaches combine overtly supportive techniques with psychoanalytic techniques and focus less clearly on the transference, the role of neutrality and the centrality of interpretation than TFP.

TFP is the most articulated psychodynamic and object relations approach to the borderline patient,[15] and has generated outcome data (see Part X, question 79). TFP is delivered in the individual format in sessions two times a week. The goal of treatment is symptom improvement and substantial change in

---

11. L. Rockland, *Supportive Therapy for Borderline Patients: A Psychodynamic Approach* (New York: Guilford Press, 1992).

12. M.M. Linehan, *Cognitive-Behavioral Treatment for Borderline Personality Disorder* (New York: Guilford Press, 1993).

13. R.J. Waldinger, "Intensive Psychodynamic Therapy with Borderline Patients: An Overview," *American Journal of Psychiatry*, 144(1987):267–274.

14. J.G. Gunderson, *Borderline Personality Disorder: A Clinical Guide* (Washington, DC: American Psychiatric Publishing, 2001), pp. 235–292.

15. J.F. Clarkin, F.E. Yeomans, & O.F. Kernberg, *Psychotherapy for Borderline Personality* (New York: John Wiley and Sons, 1999).

personality organization. As we have described earlier, since this treatment is ambitious in its goals, it should be provided to those patients with borderline organization who do not have antisocial personality disorder proper and who are not involved in massive secondary gain for illness.

Part III

TREATMENT STRATEGIES

20. What is the concept of treatment strategies?

In order to organize the therapist's understanding of how to carry out TFP, we will discuss three levels of conceptualizing the work that needs to be done. The first and broadest level involves the treatment strategies. These have to do with the long-term objectives of therapy and are based directly on the concept that integration of the patient's self-representations and object-representations will result in personality change.

The strategies are essentially guidelines to keep the therapist focused on the central task of working on the structure of the patient's internal world when, in the "real" world of the therapy session and the patient's life, the situation may appear very chaotic, because of the combination of multiple themes and problems, the possible presence of acting out, and the intense affects involved.

The treatment tactics, which are the tasks the therapist must attend to in each session, will be discussed in Part IV of this primer. The treatment techniques, which are the therapist's consistent ways of addressing what happens from moment to moment in the session, will be discussed in Part V.

The Relationship of Stategies, Tactics, and Techniques

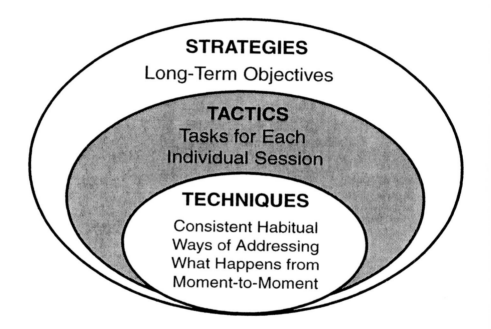

21. What are the specific treatment strategies?

Strategy I—Define the dominant object relations dyads.

Strategy II—Observe and interpret role reversals of the predominant dyads as they occur in the sessions.

Strategy III—Observe and interpret linkages between object relation dyads that defend against each other in the patient's mind, thus maintaining internal conflict and lack of integration.

Strategy IV—Elaborate and work through the more mature, integrated affective experiences that begin in the transference, and review all the patient's major relationships in the light of these changes.

All of the treatment strategies have the overall goal of integrating the split-off part-objects in order to resolve identity diffusion. We will more fully describe each strategy:

Strategy I. Define the dominant object relations dyads. This process can be subdivided into four steps:

Step A. Before being able to identify specific self- and object-representations which are present in the interaction, therapists' must allow themselves at first to *experience and tolerate the confusion of the patient's inner world* as it unfolds in the transference. Beginning therapists are sometimes anxious if they experience confusion. This is in part a response to the patient's wish that the therapist be perfect and understand everything right away. More seasoned therapists realize that this initial confusion represents empathy with the confusion of the patient's internal subjective experience.

Step B. Out of this initial confusion, therapists *develop hypotheses about how patients experience themselves and the therapist* at that point in the interaction.

Step C. The therapist proposes the dyad he has perceived to the patient. This is referred to as *naming the actors.* For example, the therapist might say:

At this point in our interaction you seem to be experiencing yourself as a helpless child who is incapable of understanding

anything and me as a rageful parent who is trying to force understanding down your throat.

Step D. The therapist then *observes the patient's response* to assess the accuracy of his hypothesis. The patient's denial of the therapist's description of the interaction does not mean it was not accurate: a vigorous, affect-laden denial can suggest confirmation as much as explicit agreement. A calm response such as "That doesn't sound right," or "I don't think that fits" is more likely evidence of an inaccurate description of the active dyad.

The treatment strategies are related to the process of interpretation (Part V, questions 50 and 51). With regard to the first strategy, if patients are not consciously aware of the roles they are attributing to the therapist and to themselves, the very act of clearly *naming the actors* can be the first step in the interpretive process insofar as it brings new awareness to patients.

Strategy II. Observe and interpret role reversals of the predominant dyads as they occur in the sessions.

Over time, sometimes within the same session and sometimes over a number of sessions, a predominant object relations dyad will reverse or "flip" in the sense that what was originally the object-representation becomes the self-representation and vice versa. Patients are not usually aware of these reversals of roles, although they are very characteristic of their interactions with others. While the therapist should be alert to these reversals and point them out when they happen, it is not always easy to notice the reversals for two reasons. First, they often occur at times of heightened affect in the session when it is difficult to "take a step back" and think clearly about the interaction. Second, the reversals often take place through the nonverbal channel, which many therapists are not as trained to track as the verbal channel.

Example: A patient asked his therapist to change a session time. When the therapist explained that she could not, the patient complained bitterly about the therapist's lack of empathy and mistreatment of him. He emphasized that he was doing his best to participate in therapy and she was thwarting him at every turn.

The active dyad here is that of the weak, powerless self being mistreated by the powerful, uncaring other. As the patient went on with his complaints, he became increasingly agitated. He got up and began to pace around the office; he stopped in front of the therapist's chair, towering over her and pointing his finger at her in a menacing way saying that people like her eventually "get what's coming to them." At that point, the therapist realized that the patient was now acting the role of the powerful, abusive other without any awareness of it. She asked him calmly if he could sit down and then pointed out to him that in the course of his actions he had become, at that moment, the type of person he was accusing her of being. The therapist empathized with the fact that it might be hard for the patient to consider this possibility because she was aware that his hatred for powerful, abusive people would make the idea that he shared any such characteristics very distasteful to him. She went on to emphasize that it is nevertheless important to be aware if he does have any such characteristics, because it is only through awareness that a person can gain control of them. In other words, if he does not like that side of him, it is only through awareness that he can master and modify it.

This example suggests why the work of therapy can be arduous and repetitious. If aspects of the patient's self are kept from his awareness, it is because the idea of those aspects is very distasteful to him, leading to *resistance to awareness*. The therapist must be alert to resistance and be prepared to focus on it as much as necessary, helping the patient see why a new way of looking at himself may be very difficult, for example:

> It is hard for you to see any feelings of hatred or aggression in you because you have such a strong aversive reaction to them. But if you look at the situation in this session, you can see that those feelings seem to be a part of you, as they are of most people. In you, however, the feelings seem to bypass your awareness and are expressed directly in your actions.

Strategy III. Observe and interpret linkages between object relation dyads that defend against each other in the patient's mind, thus maintaining internal conflict and lack of integration.

An understanding of this strategy is necessary for the therapist to interpret at a deep level since this strategy involves addressing the core of the split psyche. The presence of opposite internalized dyads is fundamental in the split internal world of the borderline patient; a dyad carrying a negative affect is opposed to and defends against a dyad carrying a positive affect. From an object relations point of view, dyads "carry" affect, drives and prohibitions in the primitively organized psyche; in normal development, these dyads evolve to form the more advanced and coherent psychological structures of ego, superego, and id.[1] This radical separation of opposing representations and affects in the primitive psyche is responsible for much of the confusion, chaos, and suffering in the lives of borderline patients. And yet, this separation exists for a reason. The core of the interpretive process is to find and explain the "motivation" for this on-going separation.

A classic example of opposing internalized dyads is found in the patient who starts therapy with a predominantly paranoid transference that is interrupted by glimpses of an intense idealized transference. In such a case, the patient presents as initially suspicious of the therapist and consequently maintains a distant, detached position in relation to him at the beginning of therapy. The patient is often defiant, saying that he can trust no one and that the only safe position in life is to have the strength to be alone. The patient expresses the belief that the therapist is exploiting him and will eventually hurt him, with accusations such as "you're just using me for income" or "you're going to make me get attached to you and then dump me" or "you want to seduce me." And yet the patient is coming to the sessions, which is already a sign of some degree of attachment. As the treatment continues, there are other

---

1. O.F. Kernberg, Object Relations Theory and Clinical Psychoanalysis (New York: Jason Aronson, 1976), pp. 34–43.

manifestations of an intense longing for attachment connected to an image of the therapist as the perfect provider. These manifestations may burst out abruptly, as in the case of a patient who appeared totally indifferent to her therapist's first vacation and then, seemingly out of the blue three months later, reacted to the news that he would be going away again by dramatically stating, "but you can't go; I can't get along without you." Alternatively, the manifestations of the defended-against dyad might appear in subtle nonverbal communications such as a yearning look in the patient's eyes even as she is saying she wants nothing to do with the therapist because she is convinced he will hurt her.

The key for the therapist is to become aware of these opposing dyads and to propose a motivation that helps understand why they must be kept apart. In the above example, the therapist might say:

> We have clear evidence that you are very suspicious of me, you are convinced I will harm you, and you are determined to remain totally independent of me. On the other hand, we also have evidence that you are longing to be close to me. There is a terrible dilemma because you can't let anyone love you. If you let yourself feel the longing you have for a good relation with me, you feel vulnerable right away—you're convinced you'll be hurt, so you flip into the defiant stance. But that's not what you really want, so, as I said, it's a real dilemma.

Strategy IV. To elaborate and work through the more mature, integrated affective experiences that begin in the transference, and to review all the patient's major relationships in the light of these changes.

It is difficult to give more than a flavor of Strategy IV since it depends on so much that has preceded it in the therapy, but the following example gives a sense of how the therapeutic dialogue takes a theme that has been central in the transference and weaves it into other relations in the patient's life:

For a long time in therapy, a patient responded with anger and threats of dropping out of treatment every time his therapist announced that he would be going away. The therapeutic work on this focused on 1) understanding the patient's difficulty attaching to others because of his conviction they did not care about him and would abandon him, and 2) the patient's attack on and destruction of his internal image of others because of this conviction. After some years of therapy, at a time when the patient was feeling "empty" because his last child got married and left home, the following exchange took place:

Patient: "You know, the last time you were away, I still felt a connection to you, but I felt sad that you weren't there. In a way, it was worse than the anger I usually feel."

Therapist: "So all those times you were enraged at me, you didn't have any sense of loss or sadness?"

Patient: "Yes, maybe that's why I'm feeling nothing now—so empty and hollow. I never wanted my kids to grow up. Now they're gone. I can understand that somebody might be angry that their kids grow up and leave home, but I could never be angry at mine—they're good kids and I love them."

Therapist: "It's interesting that you love them, but feel so empty."

Patient: "Yes, I guess I'm not feeling the love, but I know I love them."

Therapist: "I don't doubt that, but it seems you can't allow yourself other feelings toward them."

Patient: "Like the anger I'd feel at you when you went away?"

Therapist: "Your anger is too scary if it destroys the person you're angry at."

Patient: "I used to think your going away meant you didn't care about me."

Therapist: "That would be a pretty devastating thing to think about your kids."

Patient: "I never even let the thought get near me, but if I think about it, I know it's not the case."

Therapist: "So maybe you can allow yourself to miss them if you're not worried you'll get so angry at them that you'll destroy them in you."

Patient (tearful): "I guess I'm not feeling empty now. I do resent a little that they've gone away, but I still love them."

Therapist: "I know."

Part IV

TREATMENT TACTICS

22. What are the treatment tactics?

The tactics are the tasks a therapist must be aware of in each session in order to assure that the work of therapy is being carried out. Tactics involve both how to carry out the general work of therapy and how to address complications that may arise. A mastery of the tactics will both help the therapist deal with problems that arise in treating borderline patients and prevent the therapy from falling into the long unproductive periods that have led to much criticism of unfocused psychodynamic therapies. While the tactics we will discuss are common to most psychodynamic psychotherapies, certain of them must be stressed or modified in therapy with borderline patients in order to deal effectively with the confusion and chaos that can be a part of these treatments. The therapist does not usually have to use all the tactics simultaneously, but must be competent in all the tactics in order to be able to use any one of them when the material in the session calls for it. The tactics are:

1. Contract setting and maintaining the frame of treatment throughout the therapy (this helps eliminate secondary gains of illness and helps control acting out).
2. Choosing the priority theme to address in the material being presented (includes monitoring the three channels of communication, following the three principles of intervention and adhering to the hierarchy of priority of intervention).
3. Maintaining an appropriate balance between expanding incompatible views of reality between patient and therapist in preparation for interpretation and establishing common elements of shared reality.
4. Analyzing both positive and negative aspects of the transference in order to avoid missing the less obvious side of the transference.
5. Regulating the intensity of affective involvement.

Part IV-A

TACTIC #1—
CONTRACT SETTING

23. Does therapy start with the first session?

No, TFP includes two phases which precede therapy:

1. Two or three sessions (on average) to establish an accurate diagnostic impression and to obtain enough history to know what specific areas to address in the treatment contract,
2. Two or more sessions for discussion of the treatment contract. In cases where the contracting is more complicated than usual, it can take as many as five or six sessions.

At the time of the first contact with the patient (usually over the phone), the therapist should make clear that it is necessary to meet for consultation before it is possible to begin therapy. This is based on the principle that it is impossible to start treatment without a clear agreement between therapist and patient about the nature of the problems and how to address them. Taking the time for consultation can be difficult if a patient calls in crisis. In such cases, it may be necessary to refer the patient to a crisis management setting with the understanding that consultation regarding therapy can begin when the patient is out of the crisis. It is important to remember that therapy and crisis management are different forms of care. Therapists offering long-term therapy with a goal of character change should be clear in their minds that this is a specific task requiring specific conditions of treatment and that it is not only acceptable but important to maintain a boundary between the therapy they are providing and crisis management, which is provided by a separate part of the mental health services in the community. This is important for two reasons. First, it is unrealistic to believe that an individual therapist can provide the same degree of availability as the emergency services. Second, therapists who make themselves available for emergencies may end up participating in an escalating "loop of secondary gain" in which the gratification of extra contact with the therapist leads the patient to more frequent acting out.

BEGINNING TREATMENT

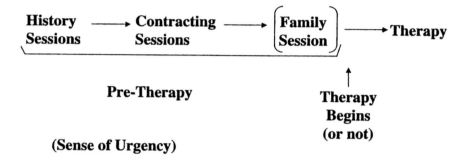

Goal: To move from <u>Acting Out</u> to <u>Transference</u>

24. What constitutes an adequate evaluation?

In addition to the standard evaluation of any new patient being considered for psychotherapy, there are a small number of key areas of assessment that require special emphasis when it comes to borderline patients. These include: 1) assessment of current or past depression, establishing a careful distinction between major depressive episodes and characterological depression, 2) assessment of the complicating co-morbid conditions sometimes present in BPD patients such as eating disorders, substance abuse, 3) evaluating the quality of the patient's interpersonal relations, 4) checking for any antisocial characteristics, and 5) careful assessment of prior treatments (including contacting prior therapists) with an emphasis on any benefit, or lack thereof, and on any ways the patient may have undermined the potential effectiveness of the prior treatment. The ways a patient might have undermined a prior treatment could range from the very concrete, such as not attending regularly or continuing to drink or take drugs, to more subtle ones, such as using the rule of free association to "flood" the therapist with an endless discourse without ever listening to or considering what the therapist says (this is a form of the defense of omnipotent control—see Part I, question 5).

25. Is it possible to include others, beside the patient, in the evaluation process?

Yes, this is an option that is left to the therapist's discretion. In the case of patients with strong antisocial characteristics, it is essential in order to verify the truth of what the patient is reporting. Otherwise, the therapist would generally decide to invite others to an evaluation session in cases where patients are very dependent on their parents, a spouse, or a partner and where the other party's involvement might have some impact on the course of the therapy. In particular, parents or partners often do not have an understanding of personality disorder and often believe that the fact of being in treatment should provide a guarantee that the patient will be all right, and, specifically, that the individual will not commit suicide. In such cases, as part of the evaluation process that precedes treatment, the therapist inquires as to the family member's understanding of the patient's condition, and then proceeds to explain this impression and its implications for treatment. This includes providing a layman's definition of personality disorders and borderline personality in particular (see question). It also includes a discussion of treatment options and the limitations of treatment.
For example:

> While I understand your concern and your wish that there could be a guarantee of a good outcome and a guarantee that your daughter not commit suicide, the state of treatment is such that I cannot provide such guarantees. In the past, long-term hospitalization provided a more comprehensive and secure level of treatment. Such treatments, for all practical purposes, do not exist now, and even they could not provide complete guarantees. Medication may have a role in your daughter's treatment, but while medication may help with some of the symptoms of the illness, it does not cure the illness itself. If you are not comfortable with what I am saying, I encourage you to consult the other forms of treatment that are available for borderline personality. I don't

know of any treatment that can provide guarantees. What I can tell you, however, is that I believe borderline personality is a treatable condition and that, with hard work in treatment, a person can get beyond it and not have to suffer from it for her whole life.

It is important to note that by making explicit that the therapist cannot guarantee the patient's life, the therapist helps to defuse any later attempts the patient may make to blackmail with threats of suicide (see question 31 for a clinical example of addressing a patient's threat of suicide in a session). Such a meeting, of course, requires the patient's consent. Should the patient refuse consent when the therapist recommends such a meeting, the therapist should explore the patient's position. If it seems that the patient is attempting to keep information out of the therapy, the therapist should generally not go ahead with the case, since the concealing of information renders effective therapy impossible.

26. What does the therapist say to the patient after arriving at a diagnostic impression?

The therapist is open about his diagnostic impression. While some patients are aware that they have a diagnosis of borderline personality, some are not. Many clinicians seem to mistakenly believe that a diagnosis of borderline personality should not be discussed with the patient. This attitude is related to the fact that the term "borderline" has taken on a pejorative meaning in most medical settings. This is unfortunate, especially because when the condition is matched with appropriate treatment, it can be treated effectively in most cases. It can be a relief for patients to hear a clear explanation of borderline personality, especially in cases where they have been told they were being treated for "depression and anxiety," a common half-truth which leaves patients confused and frustrated when they do not respond to the standard treatments for those problems.

A therapist might say to the patient:

> The evaluation suggests you have borderline personality disorder; what, if anything, does that term mean to you?

Even if the patient has some knowledge of the term, it is helpful to discuss the concept. For example:

> First, we should look at the concept of personality disorder in general. Everyone has a distinctive personality with traits that differ from one person to another. A personality becomes a personality disorder when specific traits are so exaggerated and rigid that they interfere with successful and satisfying functioning in the world. In a borderline personality, the areas of difficulty in functioning can be summarized as follows:
>
> 1.) Emotions—the individual experiences intense and quickly shifting emotions, with few periods of calm. Life is like an emotional roller coaster, with rapid shifts, extreme

highs and lows which sometimes can be mistaken for bipolar disorder, and often particular difficulty with intense anger.

2.) Interpersonal relations—these are usually chaotic and troubled. The borderline individual may have serial relationships that start with a honeymoon period and then suddenly turn bad when a disappointment is experienced. Another pattern is dramatic shifts back and forth in an ongoing relationship. In either pattern, the perceptions of self and other have a "black and white" quality. The difficulties in relationships occur with family, friends, lovers, and in work settings.

3.) Acting out—this refers to the discharge into action, rather than the conscious experiencing, of aspects of an individual's psychological world, of thoughts or feelings—it stems from the intolerance of fully experiencing emotions. Acting out can include impulsive self-destructive behaviors that sometimes are mistakenly understood as the essence of borderline personality because they are often the most dramatic feature of the disorder. It is more accurate to see these behaviors as a "red flag" pointing to the deeper difficulty— the lack of internal integration. These behaviors may take many forms, typical examples being cutting, overdosing, burning, substance abuse, promiscuous sex, and eating disorders. These behaviors are an attempt to deal with a problem, but an unsuccessful attempt. For therapy to work, it is important for the patient to refrain from these behaviors (although some slips can be tolerated) so that the emotions that contribute to them are available to work on in therapy. It is important to remember that the two ways in which affects can be shunted away from conscious awareness are through acting out, as in these impulsive behaviors, and through somatization, or experiencing the affect as a physical symptom.

4.) Identity diffusion—this is closer to the core borderline problem of lack of internal integration than the areas of difficulty listed above. Lack of a clear identity involves an individual not having a clear sense of himself, his values and his goals. This involves a sense of inner emptiness, which is related to the borderline individual's responsiveness to the immediate context and difficulty tolerating being alone. It can be, however, that the perceived emptiness may cover strong affects that are unacceptable to the individual and not allowed into his conscious awareness, the very affects that are involved in the acting out behaviors. An important part of the therapy is helping the patient gain access to these warded-off feelings and to integrate them into the person's experience of himself.

Patients who hear this description of the condition may have varied reactions, but often their response is a sense of relief that someone understands the complexity of their experience, that it is a "known quantity" and that there is a treatment designed to address it. This explanation of borderline also helps patients realize that the problem is not fundamentally one of behaviors but rather one of the underlying, automatic ways of thinking and feeling that are often out of the patient's awareness.

Some patients respond to the discussion of refraining from their destructive behaviors by saying:

> That's crazy. That shows you don't understand anything about me. I can't stop these behaviors.

The appropriate response is:

> I know that's the way you feel, and I have heard that from many other patients. I suspect, as is often the case, that neither you, nor anyone around you, has ever had the idea that you could exert some control over your behaviors, and that you may have never made a full effort to do so. In any case, it is my experience with many patients that if they tried, they could exert more control than they believed they could. You may find that this is the case with you. If it turns out that either you can't, or choose not to control your destructive impulses on most occasions, then it would be best to refer you to a type of treatment that focuses on behavioral control.

27. When is the treatment contract set with the patient?

The therapist progresses to the treatment contract when there is enough information to be confidant of the phenomenological (DSM-IV) or structural (BPO) diagnosis and to know which aspects of the patient's pathology and behavior may present a threat to carrying out the treatment. The therapist states clearly to the patient that they are moving on to the next phase of preparing for treatment:

> At this point, I have a clear enough sense of your problems and your history of dealing with them to go on to the next task we have to address in order to start therapy. We need to discuss the conditions of the treatment, that is, what it would be like—what our goals would be, the method of working on those goals, your responsibilities in the treatment, and mine. Do you have any questions before we move on to this discussion?

28. What therapeutic concepts underlie the treatment contract?

We will list the concepts behind the contract and then explain each one:[1]

I. Defining the responsibilities of the patient and the therapist.
II. Protecting the therapist's ability to think clearly and reflect.
III. Allowing the patient's dynamics to unfold in a safe place.
IV. Setting the stage for interpreting the meaning of deviations from the contract as they occur later in the therapy.
V. Providing an organizing therapeutic frame that permits therapy to become an anchor in the patient's life and that can serve as a transitional object.

I. *Defining the responsibilities of the patient and the therapist.* The therapist explains that both the therapist and the patient have responsibilities to the treatment. Those of the patient are: 1) to attend all sessions, to arrive on time and to leave at the end of the session, and to limit contact with the therapist to session times except in cases of a true emergency; 2) to pay the fee that has been agreed upon; and 3) to report all thoughts and feelings that come to mind without censoring.

The therapist's responsibilities are: 1) to provide regularly scheduled sessions and to provide adequate notice when there will be breaks or changes in the schedule; 2) to be open and attentive to all that the patient is communicating, and to make every effort to help the patient achieve a better understanding of the patient's internal world in ways that will help create change; 3) to guarantee

---

1. F.E. Yeomans, M.A. Selzer, & J.F. Clarkin, *Treating the Borderline Patient: A Contract-Based Approach*, (New York: Basic Books, 1992).

confidentiality except in a situation where breaching confidentiality may be necessary to deal with a situation of immediate threat to the patient or someone else; and 4) to provide a clearly defined therapy with the goal of character change in contrast to the type of supportive therapy or case-management which involves direct interventions in the patient's life. The principle here is that it is more useful to help the patients understand why they are having trouble solving a problem or making a decision than to participate directly in those processes.) It is important that the therapist have a clear understanding that the role of therapist is a specific one and that an individual therapist cannot be expected to perform all the services of the mental health system. It is particularly important that therapists be clear that they cannot, and should not, attempt to provide the services of the emergency room or the crisis team. It is impossible for a therapist to provide around the clock coverage. It is also unwise to communicate to patients who might harm themselves in order to have more contact with the therapist that the therapist will be available in such circumstances.

The concept of having responsibilities in therapy may be a new idea to many patients. Often, patients respond by saying:

In my other therapies, I was just told to come in and start talking.

The concept of the patient having responsibilities challenges the frequent belief of borderline patients that they will simply come to therapy and the therapist will make them better. This belief corresponds to the internal representation of the all-powerful other who can save them magically.

II. *Protecting the therapist's ability to think clearly and reflect.* This is the most important concept behind the contract. If therapists are fearful or anxious (beyond tolerable levels of countertransference which can be worked with), they cannot think clearly. In therapy with borderline patients, treatment can be overwhelmed by powerful aggressive and seductive forces. While it is essential for these forces to be in the therapy, it is also essential that they not become acted out[2] in ways that overpower or derail the therapist's efforts. The acting out of these forces is a resistance against the patient having a conscious awareness of them. In therapies where the acting out is not contained, the treatment is at risk of becoming an endless series of enactments of these forces which bars the possibility of exploring them in a way which could lead to conscious understanding, integration, and control.

For example, if the patient reacts to upsetting therapy sessions by severely cutting himself and coming repeatedly to therapy with wounds, the therapist may become more preoccupied with how to prevent further wounds than with how to understand the meaning of the interaction between patient and therapist. In addition, the affect that motivated the acting out may be temporarily lost and unavailable for exploration. The therapy then becomes derailed. The contract can help prevent this in two ways. First, by establishing the understanding that the patient make every effort to stop the destructive behavior and that, if he does not stop or decrease it significantly, his actions will necessitate a referral to a therapy focusing on behavioral control rather understanding and internal change. Second, the contract can stipulate that anytime the patient cuts himself, he must be checked by his general practitioner for any need for sutures or risk of infection before he can return to therapy. This condition of treatment *takes therapists out of the "loop" of acting out and guarantees that they not provide the secondary gain of getting more involved with the patient around the acting out.*

III. *Allowing the patient's dynamics to unfold in a safe place.* The message underlying the discussion of the contract is that all the patient's feelings are welcome in the therapeutic setting, but that certain conditions must be in place to allow the expression of the full and intense range of the patient's feelings. On the one hand,

---

2. *Acting out,* a term which has sometimes been used imprecisely in a way that confuses it with "misbehaving," actually means the expression of unconscious feelings or conflicts in actions rather than in words; acting out allows the expression of psychological material without that material passing through the individual's consciousness.

this is generally reassuring to patients since it shows that the therapist is aware of the power of the patient's internal world and has thought about how to make it possible to work with such intense feelings. On the other hand, patients may also be angry that the therapist is describing responsibilities and conditions required by the treatment—rather than offering treatment unconditionally. If the patient expresses anger at this point, the fact that the therapist can tolerate and work with the anger shows the patient "in vivo" that the therapist has the interest and ability to work with the patient's full range of feelings. To put this in technical terms, the discussion of the contract invites the early emergence of the negative transference and reassures the patient that the therapist is able to work with it.

IV. *Setting the stage for interpreting the meaning of deviations from the contract as they occur later in the therapy.* One of the tenets of psychodynamic psychotherapy is that individuals express things of which they are not conscious in a variety of ways such as slips of the tongue, somatic symptoms, fantasies, and dreams. In a similar fashion, any deviation from the frame of treatment as it is established by the contract might be the expression of material that is still unconscious. For example, a patient who starts arriving to sessions late may be expressing resistance. This resistance could be based on any number of things, from anger to love and longing which the patient may not yet be able to articulate. The essential point is that the therapist be aware of and curious (not punitive) about any deviation from the agreed-upon conditions of the treatment rather than accept the surface rationalization (e.g., a chronically late patient denying any meaning in his lateness by saying: "You know how unreliable the buses are.").

The therapist must also be attentive to any temptation on his or her part to deviate from the conditions of the treatment. Such an urge may well represent something in the countertransference. For example, if therapists are tempted to extend the time of the session, they should examine this urge, ideally before acting on it, or, if they have already acted on it, after the fact. While there may be an objectively good reason for deviating from the frame—such as to have the time to address a threat to the treatment, such as the threat of the patient dropping out of treatment, that came up at the end of the session—it may be that the therapist is enacting a countertransference reaction, which could range from guilt about ending the session to a desire to spend more time with the patient. This would be important to be aware of and to work into the therapist's understanding of the patient.

V. *Providing an organizing therapeutic frame that permits therapy to become an anchor in the patient's life and that can serve as a transitional object.* Patients who have difficulty with affective stability and stability in relationships are often concerned that two therapy sessions per week will not provide enough contact with the therapist to help them with their frequent feelings of anxiety, emptiness, and depression. Many beginning therapists who do not appreciate the power of the quickly developing transference share this concern. These therapists underestimate the power of establishing a stable, helpful object relation frame in the patient's life. While the patient's disturbing affects cannot be expected to end right away, the clearly defined therapeutic relationship helps the patient have a sense of connection to the therapist that can endure the power of extreme emotions. Patients have often reported that between sessions their thoughts of their discussions with the therapist about the treatment contract have provided a sense of connection with him or her. Those discussions communicated that the therapist knew something about their condition and was concerned and taking it seriously. Those discussions also represented the beginning of the internalization of the therapeutic dialogue that is a part of the process of getting better. For example, a patient stated:

> *I was thinking of hurting myself, then I thought about our discussion when we set up the contract. That made me feel like some kind of connection to you, even though I was angry I wasn't supposed to call you just then.*

Having said this, patients can also attack the contract as an attack on the therapist and an expression of negative transference:

I thought of cutting myself and then I thought of that idiotic contract you talk about. I said, "To hell with him if he thinks he can tell me what to do!"

In such a case, the therapist first establishes if the contract is still generally intact:

Have you decided to reject the contract we agreed on last month. . . . Have you decided to go on cutting yourself with no effort to stop?

The therapist then works on understanding the issue in terms of the contract:

The way you talk about the contract, it seems as though you experience it and me as an arbitrary authority figure trying to take control of your life for my own purposes.

Of course, patients do not always internalize the contract and the dialogue with the therapist without difficulty. It is not uncommon to hear:

As soon as I'm out of this office, it's as though you've disappeared off the face of the Earth. I try, but I can't even picture you.

It is usually helpful in these cases to interpret the patient's experience of the disappearance of the therapist as an expression of the patient's (often unconscious) anger and aggression at the therapist:

It may be that as soon as you leave this office, you attack the image you have of me in you. You might attack it because of the feeling you've reported that I'm not helping you. We've just begun to look at the extent of your wishes of what I could do for you, of the immediate help and relief you imagine I could provide if I just cared enough to do it. Your feeling that I'm not helping you, and that I could if I wanted to, might leave you very enraged at me.

29. What are the universal elements of the treatment contract?

The conditions of treatment that are common to all therapies have to do with attendance, payment, and participation (see question 28 regarding the responsibilities of the patient). Therapists sometimes feel that these are too obvious to require much attention, but experience with borderline patients shows that these parameters must be clearly defined since patients can act out around any one of them. Some patients say they see no point in coming to therapy if they are feeling good that day. Others say that they do not want to leave the house to come to a session on days when they are feeling bad. TFP requires a minimum of two forty-five minute sessions per week, although it is possible to meet three times per week. To meet only once per week would not provide adequate time for the therapist to be informed about what is going on in the patient's life and also to explore the patient's internal world through the transference.

When discussing the fact that contact is limited to session times except in the case of emergencies, it is important to define "emergency." An emergency is something out of the ordinary; it is a major event or stressor that occurs unpredictably and has a strong impact on the patient. It might be the death of a loved one, a diagnosis of cancer, or being served divorce papers. Such events would understandably be very upsetting and would justify calling the therapist and perhaps scheduling a session as soon as possible. However, borderline patients often assume that their chronic distress or suicidal feelings constitute an emergency and thus may feel free to call the therapist routinely. In setting up the contract, the therapist describes an understanding that while these feelings may be very unpleasant and painful, they unfortunately constitute part of a chronic condition. "Chronic" does not mean that the condition cannot change with treatment, but it does mean that the painful affects and suicidal feelings are present on a regular basis and may continue for some time before change takes place. The fact that the patient experiences these feelings regularly distinguishes them from an emergency. Dealing with these feelings is one of the major objectives of treatment but will take time. If a patient reacts to dysphoric feelings with self-destructive or suicidal actions, specific treatment parameters must be set up in the contract to address those problems, as discussed in the next question.

30. What are the elements of the contract that are specific to the individual patient?

Setting up the contract around threats to the treatment that are unique to a particular patient requires more skill and judgment on the part of the therapist than dealing with the universal elements of the contract. The therapist first determines what past behaviors or elements of the patient's history are likely to threaten the continuity and success of the current treatment and then establishes adequate parameters to address these threats. It is important to mention that while we speak of "threats to the treatment," we did not mean that the patient consciously sets out to undermine or destroy the treatment. It is rather that even though the patient's split psychological structure is primitive in nature, it is nonetheless a defense geared to protect the patient from the anxiety of having split-off aggressive drives contaminate or destroy libidinally-invested objects [i.e., the bad object destroy the good one]. Insofar as therapy calls on the patient to experience and express all feelings, it can threaten the fragile homeostasis of the split psyche. A patient might instinctively attack or flee this process. The contract is meant to anticipate and address these eventualities.

The following is a list of common threats to the treatment; it is not all-inclusive and the therapist should be on the lookout for other possible threats when evaluating the patient:

1. Suicidal and self-destructive behaviors
2. Homicidal impulses or actions, including threatening the therapist
3. Lying or withholding of information
4. Substance abuse
5. Uncontrolled eating disorder
6. Excessive phone calls or other intrusions into the therapist's life
7. Not paying the fee or arranging not to be able to pay
8. Problems created external to the sessions that interfere with the therapy

9. A chronically passive lifestyle which, although not immediately threatening, would defeat any therapeutic effort toward change in favor of the continued secondary gain of illness

It is important to address these threats and discuss the plan for dealing with them before beginning the actual therapy. The agreement on how to deal with these threats once again calls on the patient to accept some responsibility in the treatment. An example of this is how *suicidal ideation and behaviors* will be addressed in the treatment (see question 31).

The parameters to be set in place are more specific according to how concrete and tangible the threat to the treatment is. For example, *patients' withholding of information* is harder to get a handle on than patients' starving themselves. In the former situation, the therapist is generally limited to emphasizing to the patient that withholding information makes effective treatment impossible, and that, while it may not be detected right away, the withholding of information eventually becomes apparent (the exception to this is when the patient presents with severe, chronic lying and the therapist may have to establish a system of checking with a third party, such as a parent or spouse, at times to verify what the patient is saying).

More specific, behavioral parameters may be set in response to a threat such as an eating disorder. With *anorexics,* a minimum safe weight must be established in conjunction with a dietician or eating disorders specialist. The patient must agree to being weighed regularly by that person with the understanding that if the weight should fall below the minimum, TFP will be suspended in favor of a pure eating disorders treatment until the weight is again in the safe range.

With regard to *substance abuse,* it is advisable to insist on a period of at least six months of sobriety with mandatory participation in a Twelve Step program before starting TFP. Periodic drug screens may be a part of the contract for a patient with a history of substance abuse.

Problems created external to the session can be subtle to discern. These include such conditions as patients who start skipping classes with the knowledge that their parents will only pay for treatment if they stay in school, or patients who incite their boyfriend or girlfriend to make threatening calls to the therapist by implying that the therapist disapproves of their relationship. In either case, the therapist must make clear to the patient that these behaviors pose a threat to the treatment and that must take responsibility for the potential threat.

The problem of patients who lead a *chronically passive lifestyle* is one which therapists have traditionally been reluctant to address. However, the goal of TFP is character change and, therefore, better functioning. It is not a "maintenance" treatment and does not see borderline pathology as justification for abandoning efforts to have an active role in the world. In cases where patients have adopted the patient role as a way of life and, in the most severe cases, have settled into the disability system, the therapist explains that in order to be effective, therapy requires the patient to be engaged in an active life. This could be in the form of studies, a full or part-time job, volunteer work, or, in the most severe cases, a day program. In addition to addressing the acting out of a passive, dependent, entitled role, patients' engaging in some form of activity places them in situations which may bring into focus interpersonal difficulties arising from their internal object relations.

31. How do I keep anxiety about the possibility of patients' killing themselves from distracting me from my work?

Borderline patients' *suicidal ideation, threats, and actions* can have a powerful effect on therapists, often leading otherwise skilled therapists to deviate from standard practice, and from the treatment frame, in ways which usually "backfire." Most typically, borderline patients yearn for proof of love and concern, and may demand more and more time and attention from the therapist as a form of proof. If the therapist attempts to meet these demands rather than interpret them, the patient generally responds with an escalation of demands (since no caretaking is perfect and no proof is adequate); this escalation often includes suicidal threats. Since the patient's demand is based on a primitive internal representation of an all-good, all-powerful, and all-available provider, any shortcoming on the part of the therapist may be experienced as an intentional, even sadistic, withholding, and as a sign that the therapist does not care about the patient and/or is rejecting the patient. This experience of the therapist can justify, in the mind of the patient, an aggressive response, including suicidal threats or actions.

Thus, in order to defuse the potential power of suicidality in the interaction between patient and therapist, it is important to address this issue first in the contract at the beginning of therapy and then with interpretation when the material comes up. The essential point in discussing suicidality is that, while *discussion* of these feelings is welcome in the context of the therapy, issues of suicidal *intent or actions* are not within the realm of a psychotherapy treatment, but must be dealt with in the emergency services segment of the health care system. This position is sometimes criticized as a shirking of responsibility by the therapist. However, it can be argued that it is irresponsible for the therapist to pretend to provide a level of security and protection that is not realistically possible. In our experience, therapists create problems more often by offering themselves as available for emergency intervention and then not having the necessary resources than by making clear what the limits of their involvement are and when a patient must have access to a different level of intervention.

In discussing suicidality, the first order of business is to distinguish between that which is characterological in nature (when suicidal ideation is part of a "way of life") and that which occurs in the context of a major depressive episode or psychotic illness.[3] This is especially important because many borderline patients have had concurrent episodes of major depressive illness.[4] In contracting about suicidality, the therapist must make it clear that suicide as part of a major depressive episode or psychosis would require a shift from the ongoing therapy to a treatment modality such as medication or hospitalization if necessary.

Having made this diagnostic issue clear, the principle behind the contract regarding characterological suicidality is to place the therapist in a position outside of the patient's "loop of acting out." That is, the therapist will retain the role as TFP therapist and will not switch into the role of crisis team, crisis manager, or emergency room psychiatrist in response to the patient's suicidality. The discussion of contracting around suicidality can be summarized in the following flow chart:

As discussed above (Part II, question 18), it is important that therapists working with borderline patients be able to accept the possibility that patients can kill themselves. To not be able to accept this possibility would leave therapists in positions where they could be controlled by a patient's threats of suicide. To be controlled by the patient makes therapy impossible and does not provide any assurance of the patient's survival. In fact, therapists who respond to patients' attempts to control them could make the

---

3. O.F. Kernberg, "The Suicidal Risk in Severe Personality Disorders: Differential Diagnosis and Treatment," *Journal of Personality Disorders* 15 (2001): 195–208.

4. M. Swartz, D. Blazer, L. George, & I. Winfield, "Estimating the Prevalence of Borderline Personality Disorder in the Community," *Journal of Personality Disorders* 4 (1990): 257.

Contract Around Suicidal Behavior in a Chronically Suicidal Borderline Patient
Patient feels the urge to kill self between therapy sessions

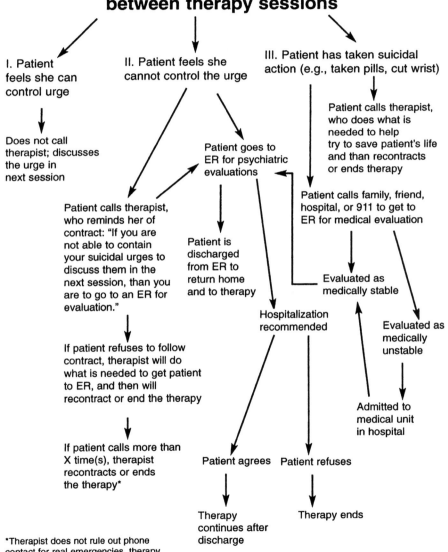

I. Patient feels she can control urge

Does not call therapist; discusses the urge in next session

II. Patient feels she cannot control the urge

Patient calls therapist, who reminds her of contract: "If you are not able to contain your suicidal urges to discuss them in the next session, than you are to go to an ER for evaluation."

If patient refuses to follow contract, therapist will do what is needed to get patient to ER, and then will recontract or end the therapy

If patient calls more than X time(s), therapist recontracts or ends the therapy*

Patient goes to ER for psychiatric evaluations

Patient is discharged from ER to return home and to therapy

Hospitalization recommended

Patient agrees

Therapy continues after discharge

Patient refuses

Therapy ends

III. Patient has taken suicidal action (e.g., taken pills, cut wrist)

Patient calls therapist, who does what is needed to help try to save patient's life and than recontracts or ends therapy

Patient calls family, friend, hospital, or 911 to get to ER for medical evaluation

Evaluated as medically stable

Evaluated as medically unstable

Admitted to medical unit in hospital

*Therapist does not rule out phone contact for real emergencies, therapy ends when a pattern of breeches shows that the patient is not serious about adhering to the contract.

risk of suicide even greater since there will inevitably be the point at which therapists cannot respond to patients' wish for perfect care. If, at that point, patients still think they can control the therapist to obtain this perfect care, they may escalate their suicidality.

A brief clinical example of dealing with a suicidal threat in the course of therapy is as follows. A patient who was angry that her therapist was going away stated:

> *If you don't cancel your plans and stay here, I'll kill myself, and it'll be your fault.*

The therapist replied:

> **As you know, I've always said there is a risk that you will kill yourself. I hope you won't, but, whatever happens, there's one thing I can be sure of. That is, if you do kill yourself, that will be a choice you make and there is no way it could be considered "my fault."**

After some discussion, the patient acknowledged that it made no sense to claim that her therapist would be responsible if she acted on her angry impulse.

32. What about patients who call very frequently?

Borderline patients sometimes exhaust well-intentioned therapists by calling frequently and at all hours. The exhaustion comes both from the frequency of the calls and the feeling that no matter how much time the therapist spends on the phone with the patient, it is never enough. The therapist usually feels anxious and worried after hanging up. Again, satisfying the patient's demand is impossible if the patient is searching for the perfect provider and experiences anything less than unlimited availability as indifference and abandonment. While some calls are appropriate (see Part IV-A, question 29 regarding emergencies, and question 33), many calls of distress are enactments of the particular dynamic: "I want you to be there for me/I know you won't." They are expressions of the fundamental conflict between a wish for the perfect provider and the angry certainty of disappointment. Seen in this light, it is not helpful to be available for such calls. It is more therapeutic to establish clear parameters around phone calls and to deal with the urge to call, or calls made in violation of the parameters, with an interpretation along the lines of:

> In your previous therapy, you called Dr. X. frequently, but this did not lead to any real improvement. Rather than repeat that pattern, it would be more helpful to understand what you seem to be playing out in those calls. On the one hand, you wish for someone who could provide you with perfect caretaking. However, no matter how available a caretaker may be, they fall short of perfection and leave you with the conviction you are uncared for and can trust no one. It is important to see how your insistence on a perfect provider who does not exist in the real world leads you to reject the real help that is available, leaving you feeling alone and abandoned.

33. What calls are appropriate?

Appropriate calls fall into two categories:

1. Calls to deal with practical issues such as the need to cancel a session or reschedule; and

2. True emergencies: these are defined as situations which are unpredictable and highly stressful which could understandably justify communication with the therapist before the next session. As discussed in question 29, some examples are the death of a loved one, being diagnosed with a serious illness, or being involved in an accident. Some discussion over the phone or setting up an extra appointment may be appropriate under such circumstances.

It is again important to note that the chronic distress, self-destructive, and suicidal impulses common in borderline patients do not constitute an emergency. This is precisely because they are a chronic condition that patients must agree to manage to the best of their ability while the ongoing therapy addresses the underlying problems. As delineated in the flow chart in question 31, patients are expected to seek emergency services if they are not able to control these impulses rather than expect that the therapist can provide such services. Once again, this is based both on the reality that emergency services will provide better emergency care than an individual practitioner and also on the *concept of interrupting loops of secondary gain in which patient is rewarded for acting out by getting more contact with the therapist.*

34. What is done if the patient breaks the treatment contract?

When a patient breaks the contract, the therapist must do two things: 1) set a limit with regard to the violation of the contract, and 2) explore and try to interpret the meaning of the violation. The balance between these two tasks differs according to the degree to which the patient is still in agreement with, versus rejects, the conditions of the contract. If the patient appears to have "slipped" in breaking the contract and is still in basic agreement with it, the therapist may proceed more quickly to the exploration. For example, if the therapist has established that the patient's agreement with the contract is still in place, it is appropriate to move on to exploring the meaning of the break:

> Since you're saying you agree that scratching yourself was a slip and you're still committed to trying to resist those urges, let's look what scratching yourself yesterday might have meant.

If, on the other hand, the patient is acting and talking in a way that communicates a rejection of the contract, the therapist must focus on seeing if it is possible to reestablish the contract before proceeding to explore the meaning of the break. In such cases, the therapist may have to point out that the patient is creating the situation of choosing between therapy and that particular form of acting out. For example:

> You tell me now that you've been drinking every night for the past week. By doing so, you're creating a situation where the options are clear. First, you can stop drinking. . . . You can still do that safely without requiring a detox program. If you choose this, and you will have to be totally honest about it, then we can continue the therapy with a priority being to understand what it means that you were doing this and not

telling me about it. However, you may choose to continue drinking. In that case, you are choosing drinking over therapy. While I think this choice would be a tragedy, it is one you could make. To continue therapy under those circumstances would be pointless since your drinking would undermine any possibility that therapy help you. If you choose drinking over therapy, I will give you referrals to alcohol treatment services in our area and I hope you will use them. I remind you, though, that it would be you, not I, who would be ending the therapy.

There are also intermediate situations where the patient's behavior does not present an immediate threat to the treatment, but would pose a threat if it continued unabated. The principle here is that if there is any evidence of a pattern of behavior that would undermine the therapy over time, the therapist must point out that if the behavior does not stop, it would make any effective therapy impossible. It is important in such cases to focus on *the pattern* rather than an isolated occurrence. An example of this would be repeated attendance problems:

We have to talk about your attendance here. We meet for two or three times, then you miss the next couple of sessions. This pattern is making it impossible for us to have any continuity in our work and if this continues, we'll have to acknowledge that this arrangement isn't working and look for some alternative treatment that might be more suited to you. Of course, we should try to understand what is motivating this behavior in you, but if it continues for the next month, that will be tantamount to your letting me know that either you are not interested in this treatment, or that, for whatever reason, you can not do it.

It should be noted that even in cases where the patient seems very resistant to therapy, it is common that an attachment (although perhaps a conflicted one) to the therapist has developed (see Part VII, question 64A). It sometimes surprises therapists that when a patient with a long history of acting out is given the choice of continuing the acting out or continuing in therapy, the patient chooses the therapy (although it can be a "rocky road" before the acting out is completely stopped).

35. When and how does a therapist shift from the contract-setting phase of therapy to the therapy itself?

When the therapist feels that the patient has expressed adequate agreement[5] with the arrangements and parameters described in the contract, the therapist marks the transition to therapy by saying:

> I think we have discussed your difficulties and the treatment approach I recommend enough to begin the therapy. So, unless you have any further questions, we can start. In other words, this is the point where I stop structuring the sessions by asking questions and discussing the conditions of treatment with you. We proceed now by your reporting what comes to your mind.

---

5. It is unrealistic to expect perfect agreement; in fact, a therapist should be suspicious of the sincerity of a patient who expresses perfect agreement to the contract with no reservations or hesitation.

36. What are the most common ways therapists have to intervene to protect the treatment frame?

The need to protect the frame of treatment can vary greatly from one case to another. Threats to the frame include all the ways in which patients may not live up to their responsibilities in the treatment (see Part IV-A, question 28), any of the specific threats that could require contracting (see Part IV-A, question 30), and ways in which patients may induce the therapists to deviate from their role. As stated above, protecting the frame involves both addressing threats to the treatment and exploring the meaning of the threats.

Common threats to the frame are attendance problems, withholding information, dropping out,[6] and the resumption of substance abuse or eating disorder symptoms.

A more subtle form of threatening the frame occurs when patients attempt to induce therapists to deviate from their roles. Patients often agree to the principles of TFP and then act in ways designed to engage the therapist as an active helper in their life rather than as an expert trained to help them change the underlying problem in personality structure. An example is the patient who had made a suicide attempt because of having failed the previous semester at school and who begins to focus on her wish that the therapist give her practical help in the form of going over her homework with her:

> *You know I can't do this on my own. . . . I just can't. I can see it happening again. I'm not getting the work done, I'll fail and I'll try to*

---

6. Dropping out may sound like the end of the treatment more than a threat to the treatment. However, borderline patients who have terrible ambivalence about attachment are prone to repeatedly "dropping out" of therapy. We put this term in quotes because the patient's statement that she is dropping out is more often an expression of how difficult she is finding it to stay involved with the therapist. If this situation is handled appropriately (see Part VIII, question 65) most drop outs can be avoided. Unfortunately, many therapists do not understand the dynamics of the situation and do not intervene in the way that would be most likely to avoid the drop out.

kill myself again, and maybe this time I'll really do it. If someone came to me with such a clear and simple need for help, and I knew that person's life depended on it, I'd do something! I wouldn't sit there like you do. Are you crazy? Are you heartless? Do you want me to kill myself?

The temptation for the therapist to provide practical support is great, and the risk of doing so may seem small, but it is not. First, if the therapist intervened with "practical help," the therapist would be joining the patient in her belief that she was incapable of doing her studies [the initial diagnostic phase revealed no deficit in intelligence and no history of learning disability]. In this sense, the therapist would be entering the patient's internal world rather than helping her to observe it. The therapist would be entering as the (for the moment) idealized helper desired by the needy, helpless representation of the self. This enactment of a superficial part of the patient's internal world would be likely to soon be undercut by a deeper level in which the patient thwarted the therapist's efforts, thereby "proving" that no one is there for her. In addition to this, the therapist would miss the opportunity to explore the aspect of the internal world getting played out in the transference—the dramatic enactment of the patient's experience of the other as failing her, even though the therapist is providing exactly the type of help described when they set up the treatment.

37. What is the concept of secondary gain and why is it important to eliminate it?

From a psychoanalytic point of view, the primary gain of a symptom or condition is the relief from anxiety that it provides, as in the classic example of a hysterical conversion symptom (see Part I, question 6). The secondary gain is any benefit the patient may experience from the symptom or condition beyond that primary intrapsychic relief. Secondary gain could range from the gratification patients experience from contact with their therapist to psychiatric disability benefits received from the government because of their borderline condition. It is important to be aware of any secondary gain since it runs counter to efforts to get better. Some patients seem to replace an active, independent life with participation in various forms of treatment. The psychiatric disability payments some patients receive may discourage them from making efforts to become self-supporting. These issues of secondary gain are generally discussed in the contract-setting phase of treatment. The therapist makes it clear that the treatment is to support more autonomous functioning so that, except in extreme cases for limited periods of time, the therapist would not support psychiatric disability and would make functioning at some level at work or in school an expectation of the treatment.

The more subtle forms of secondary gain may come up in the course of treatment around the gratification the patient experiences from the therapist's attention. While it may be unspoken, the therapist sometimes may sense a developing complacency in the patient, a feeling of accepting the status quo and not putting any energy into the effort to change. It may be that the satisfaction the patient experiences from being with the therapist has become the main reason for coming to therapy. The therapist should explore this possibility. Like most threats to the frame, it has transference implications and reflects an aspect of the patient's internal world. The therapist might say:

> My sense lately is that you're quite comfortable in the therapy and that, although you bring up problems you're

having, you're not listening much to what I say or seeming to work on it or think about it. This makes me think that the fact of coming here and telling me about your problems is gratifying in itself. If this is the case, we've got to look at it because this therapy is meant to help you change, not to merely to provide some relief from your current state. It might help to consider the fact that, to simplify for the sake of argument, people come to therapy for one of two reasons: the first is to change, and the second is because it feels good to be with someone who pays attention and listens to you. Of course, in real life people might come for a combination of the two reasons. But the important thing is that it seems that more and more you are here because you like the experience of being here. The fact that you haven't been paying much attention to what I say would fit with the idea that you want to just be in therapy indefinitely, maybe even resisting the process of change so the therapy will never end. I point this out because it helps us understand something about you, that you have a wish to turn me into a kindly companion who sits and listens to you. But if we let this situation go on, without taking note of it and using the information to help you change, then we're abandoning our therapy, with its goal of change. What I recommend we do at this point is to explore further your wish to be taken care of, to try to understand the role this wish plays in your life, and to understand why you have not been able to get any satisfaction of this wish outside of treatment situations where it is the other person's official role to take care of you, at least to some degree.

Often the exploration of the wish to be taken care of in people who use treatment to that end reveals an underlying dyad of a suspicious self who does not trust that anyone would ever have a genuine interest in that person and who, thus, must turn to structured caretaking situations to make up for what the person believes cannot be found in real life.

Part IV-B

CHOOSING THE PRIORITY
THEME TO ADDRESS

38. Given the amount of data therapists are exposed to in a session, how do they decide what to address?

Choosing which material to address is one of the most important questions for therapists dealing with borderline patients because they are exposed to so much material that often they do not know what to begin to focus on. In our discussion of choosing which material to address, we will review the following major concepts:

1. The economic, dynamic and structural principles of intervention,
2. The three channels of communication, and
3. The hierarchy of priorities with regard to the material presented in a given session.

39. What are the economic, dynamic, and structural principles that guide the therapist's attention?

These principles are based on psychoanalytic concepts involving the dynamic forces at work within the mind—the interaction of drives, affects, prohibitions, and external reality.

The term *economic principle* refers to the notion of the economy of forces in the psyche. The practical application of this principle in carrying out therapy is that the therapists should *focus their attention on the material carrying the most affect* in the session. This may appear self-evident at times, such as when the patient is discussing his or her mother's diagnosis of cancer with intense affect. However, it could be that a patient brings up the mother's diagnosis of cancer, but in the same session speaks with more affect about being late for work that day. The therapist should first inquire and explore the affect.

The *dynamic principle* considers the dynamic forces in conflict in the psyche and how they are represented by object relations dyads. This principle is used primarily in determining the order in which the therapist addresses material in making an interpretation. In practical terms, therapists can ask themselves:

What is defending against what?

and should generally choose interventions to address the defensive level before addressing the impulse being defended against. This is called *working from surface to depth* in the sense that the defense is more close to conscious awareness. An example of this would be:

> **You are very insistent on seeing me as cold and depriving in a sadistic way. Even when I offered you an alternative session because you cannot come on Monday, you harshly responded that I was only offering one alternative that was convenient for me. I have noticed that your depiction of me as cold and withholding has increased over the past weeks. Can we agree that this is the way you have been seeing me?**

This intervention is describing the dyad that is serving the defensive function. If the patient agrees, the therapist could continue:

It seems this intensification of seeing me this way could be covering up other feelings you are having which you are uncomfortable with and which make you very anxious. In subtle ways, such as the look in your eyes at times, you seem to be experiencing me differently. These subtle signs suggest you may be feeling something positive in regard to me, but for some reason this appears to make you anxious, resulting in a stepping up in your criticisms of me, as though to reassure yourself that nothing positive could exist between you and me.

The therapist is beginning to address the affect and impulse being defended against. The final step in this process would be to understand the need to defend against these feelings. (There will be more discussion of these issues in Part V, question 51).

The *structural principle* is a broad organizing principle reminding the therapist to try to formulate and maintain an overview of the predominant structure of intrapsychic forces as they are represented in borderline patients by the dominant object relations dyads and, as they are represented in neurotic patients, by the more organized structures of id, ego, and superego. In borderline patients, the most effective way of arriving at this formulation is to determine the *chronic, baseline transference* which underlies the shifting transferences observed from moment to moment and which represents the principle conflict at a given phase of the therapy. Although it is not always the case, most borderline patients begin therapy with a chronic paranoid transference, that is, with a self-representation of a weak, vulnerable self who is on guard against any feelings of closeness that they may develop because of the belief that the object will inevitably reject, abandon, hurt, or exploit him (see Part II, question 17).

In summary, these three principles remind the therapist to: 1) follow the patient's affect as an indicator of what the predominant object relation dyad is likely to be at a given moment, 2) look for and address first the material that seems to be serving a defensive purpose, and 3) look for the overall organization of dyads in terms of what surface dyad is defending against what underlying dyad (this concept will be discussed again in Part V, question 51.)

40. What are the three channels of communication?

1. The verbal content of the patient's discourse, or simply put, what the patient says.
2. The patient's nonverbal communication: how patients say what they say (tone of voice, speech volume, etc.) and patients' body language (posture, facial expressions, gestures, eye contact, etc.).
3. The therapist's countertransference, which may be the most subtle channel of communication. Countertransference is defined as the therapist's total emotional reaction to the patient at every point in time. It is a complex phenomenon in that it is determined by four factors:

a) The patient's transference to the therapist,
b) The patient's objective reality (the therapist may be concerned about or have other reactions to the circumstances of the patient's life),
c) The therapist's own transference dispositions as determined by his or her internal world (it is because of this aspect of countertransference that a therapist must be aware of his or her own habitual reactions. In order to insure such awareness, it is advisable for therapists to have had their own psychoanalysis or psychotherapy), and
d) The reality of the therapist's life (e.g., is the therapist's practice "slow," and is there pressure to "keep" a case because of the income involved?).

The fact that these four influences all impact on the therapist's countertransference makes it essential to try to distinguish the source(s) of internal experience in relation to the patient. Countertransference is a particularly important source of information in working with borderline patients. Clinical experience shows that *the more severe the patient's character pathology, the more the patient's transference determines the therapist's countertransference.*

Consequently, in borderline patients, much of the countertransference is determined by the patient's internalized object relations dyads as they emerge in the transference.

Countertransference may either be concordant or complementary.[1] Concordant countertransference occurs when the therapist experiences an affective identification with the patient's current subjective affective experience (which the patient may be more or less clearly aware). In other words, the therapist experiences empathy with the patient's subjective experience. In this case, there is communication between the patient's current self-representation and the therapist's empathy. One could say that when the therapist experiences concordant countertransference, the therapist learns how the patient feels through a trial identification.

Complementary countertransference is rather an identification with the object representation included in the currently active dyad. A complementary countertransference may provide a better feel for the patient's split-off internal objects, and thus, for the totality of the current dyad.

An example will help clarify these concepts. If a patient says, "I failed my test." and then remains silent, the therapist might feel sad. This would represent a concordant countertransference, in which case the therapist might say:

It may be that you're silent because you think this is the end of the world.

However, in the same situation, the therapist might feel angry. This would represent a complementary countertransference, in which case the therapist might say:

It may be that you're silent because you think I might be critical of you.

---

1. H. Racker, "The Meaning and Uses of Countertransference," *Psychoanalytic Quarterly* 26 (1957): 303–357.

In this case, the therapist realizes that the anger is an identification with the persecutory object the patient projects in the transference.

Of course, therapists who are treating non borderline patients should also be aware of the three channels. *However, as a general rule, the more primitive the pathology, the more important are the second and third channels—the nonverbal and the countertransference.* Simply put, this is because of the split internal world of the borderline patient. In general, patients are already aware of what they are saying at any given point but are not aware of the internal contradictions or of split-off parts which never pass through their awareness but are only expressed through action or somatization.[2] *This is extremely important for the therapist to realize. Therapists who are trained to listen carefully to the patient's associations but who are not attuned to precise and subtle observation of the patient's interaction with the therapist and of the countertransference can go on for long periods without making any progress in therapy.*

---

2. A. Green, *On Private Madness* (Madison, CT: International Universities Press, 1993), p. 209.

41. What is the hierarchy of priorities with regard to the material presented in a session?

This hierarchy lists the issues that are likely to come up in a session and prioritizes the order in which they should be addressed when they come up. The hierarchy is based on two main principles:

1. First, address any *threats to carrying out the treatment*, including threats to the patient's life or safety;

2. Then address any *manifestations of the self and object representations in the patient's internal world* as expressed in the transference or other material.

The threats must be addressed first because they are obstacles to the more central work of understanding the patient's internal world.

The hierarchy of priorities with regard to content of the session:

I. Obstacles to transference exploration
   a.) Suicidal or homicidal threats
   b.) Overt threats to treatment continuity (e.g., requests to decrease session frequency, indications of imminent drop out)
   c.) Dishonesty or deliberate withholding in sessions (e.g., lying, refusing to discuss certain subjects, silences occupying most of the sessions)
   d.) Contract breaches (e.g., failure to maintain required weight, failure to attend AA meetings and maintain sobriety, refusal to take prescribed medication)
   e.) In-session acting out (e.g., throwing objects, damaging office furnishing, shouting so loud it disturbs people in adjoining offices, refusing to leave at the end of the session)
   f.) Nonlethal acting out between sessions
   g.) Monopolizing the time in sessions with trivial themes devoid of affect ("trivialization")

II. Transference manifestations leading to delineation of self and object representations
   a) Verbal references to the therapist
   b) The patient's "way of being" with the therapist (this includes the patient's manner at any given moment, the patient's tone and attitude, and the patient's physical communication, such as sitting in a seductive manner)
   c) The therapist's inferences as to transference manifestations (e.g., references to other doctors, authority figures, etc.)
III. Nontransferential affect-laden material
   This includes discussion of people and situations in the patient's life outside of the therapy setting (although, very often, exploration of this material leads back to transference issues; the therapist's best guide to the transference implications of such material is to periodically think about "Why is this person telling me this material right now?")

42. How does the therapist use this hierarchy from moment to moment in the course of a session?

It is important for therapists to become so familiar with this list that it becomes "second nature" in their thinking as they are listening to and observing all the material in the session. *The hierarchy may lead the therapist to interrupt the patient's flow of associations.* For example, a patient may mention suicidal ideation in passing and move on to other material. The therapist, attentive to priorities, will intervene with a comment such as:

> **You said something about suicide without making it clear what the story about that is. It's important to clarify if that poses a risk to your life and to our work together right now before we can go on to explore any other issue. Of course, it's also important to try to understand what the meaning of your reporting suicidal ideation is at this point.**

Similarly, anorexic patients who have agreed in the treatment contract to maintain a certain weight may come to sessions appearing increasingly thin while making no verbal reference to their eating habits. It is the therapist's responsibility to address this contract breach before going on with the "business as usual" of addressing other material.

The hierarchy of priorities has much in common with the possible threats to the treatment discussed in the contract setting (see Part IV-A, question 30). In that sense, the therapist's technique in following the hierarchy of priorities recalls the type of thinking employed in setting up the contract. Whenever a threat to the treatment arises in a session, the therapist should recall the parameters established in the contract for dealing with that threat. If a threat emerges in the course of treatment that was not predicted in the contract, the therapist must first establish parameters with the patient for dealing with that threat and, once the parameters have been agreed upon, proceed with the work of exploring the meaning of the material. *It is an important rule of therapy that it is only after parameters are in place that the work of exploration can go on. Once the parameter is established the therapist should proceed with the question:*

Now we can try to understand that at this point in our working together why this issue has come up that has threatened our work.

For example, if a patient reports what sounds like serious suicidal ideation in the course of treatment, the therapist must first rule out the presence of a major depressive episode and then remind the patient of their initial agreement for dealing with suicidal ideation (see Part IV-A, question 31). Only then can the work of exploring the meaning of the patient bringing this up at this time be explored.

43. Which items on this list generally present a special challenge to the therapist?

Therapists are often unsure of how to address the issue of nonlethal acting out. This is a broad category that includes, but is not limited to, superficial cutting, head-banging, hair-pulling, "playing around" with the dose of medication, periodic substance abuse "slips," and calling in sick to work. The principles that guide the vigorousness of the therapist's response to these forms of acting out are:

1. How great a risk does the behavior pose?
2. Does the behavior make the therapist so uncomfortable that he or she is unable to think clearly?
3. Does the acting out "siphon off" affects from the sessions to a degree that renders the deep exploration of the patient's internal world impossible?

Dealing with nonlethal acting out can be more challenging for the therapist than dealing with potentially lethal acting out. Suicidal ideation that the patient cannot control shifts the treatment to an emergency or inpatient setting. When the risk of lethal action is over, the exploratory therapy can begin again. However, superficial cutting is not generally cause for shifting the treatment to an emergency setting. The therapist's attitude should be that the nonlethal acting out is not only detrimental in concrete ways such as leaving scars in the case of cutting or, to take another example, risking losing a job by missing days at work, but it is also detrimental to the work of therapy because it deprives therapy of the affects which constitute the "raw material" of therapy (recall the definition of *acting out*, Part IV-A, question 28). What would the patient *have felt* if he did not cut himself, or if he had gone to work? The therapist's response to continued nonlethal acting out should be:

> Your continuing to cut yourself when you get upset may seem to solve the problem of your anxiety, but it is not a very

successful solution to the problem. For one thing, it leaves you with scars. But, more importantly from the viewpoint of our work together, it robs us of the material we need to work on here. That quick discharge of your feelings takes away the intense affects we need to work with in your sessions. If you continue to deal with your feelings in this way—by discharging them in actions—we will not be able to accomplish the work we have set out to do. It's very important for you to understand that continued acting out of this nature is not compatible with our work here.

If the patient continues the acting out on a regular basis, the therapist may have to point out that the patient is making an exploratory therapy impossible and that his continued acting out behavior is an indication for referral to a treatment focused on addressing problematic behaviors. In discussing this situation, the therapist will, of course, suggest that the continued acting out may be a way of avoiding any awareness of the related affects and meaning. Sometimes this discussion of referral to another therapy is enough to motivate the patient to stop or significantly decrease acting out. Making the decision to refer the patient to another treatment is a challenge for the therapist because it requires a clinical judgment as to when acting out interferes so severely with the exploratory process as to render it impossible. There is no absolute objective guideline for this decision. Even though most patients demonstrate a significant decrease in acting out during the first six to twelve months of therapy, in some cases it can continue to be an issue much further into treatment.

44. Is there a strict separation between the addressing obstacles to therapy and the analytic work itself?

No, one of the interesting things about psychoanalytically-based therapy is that working with the resistance to therapy always provides some information relevant to the patient's psychological processes. For example, in the case of a patient who threatens to drop out of treatment, it is important to first address the threat, and then to try to understand what fear it might represent. The therapist might say:

> Your increasing talk about being bored here and thinking it's not worth your time or money to keep coming here presents a serious issue. It's true that after three months of therapy you do not feel a lot better and, in fact, report that you feel more anxious in some ways. It may also be true that you are feeling bored here, although from my observation you appear uncomfortable and anxious. We can get back to that later, but the first thing to address is if you're going to keep coming or if you'll stop. You are, of course, free to do what you chose, but I think it's important to let you know my point of view on this. I think it would be a big mistake for you to stop therapy. I believe there are feelings behind this wish which you may not be clear of, but we don't have any chance of trying to understand those feelings if you end the therapy. Therefore, I think we first have to have an understanding that you will not act on your thoughts about ending therapy without first taking some time here to discuss it. In other words, if you are tempted between sessions simply not to come back, I strongly recommend that you come here so we can more fully discuss all the feelings in you that may be pushing you in this direction. Do you agree with that?

According to whether the patient agrees or not, the therapist would proceed differently. The reader is referred to the later section on interpretation (see Part V, questions 50 and 51) for advice on how to proceed in a situation like this. The current example is offered here to illustrate how an obstacle to the treatment may become the starting point for further exploration and understanding of the patient's internal world.

Part IV-C

THE REMAINING TACTICS

45. How does the therapist maintain the balance between expanding incompatible views of reality between patient and therapist and establishing common elements of reality?

The general approach in TFP is to have patients elaborate their view of the world and, in particular, of the therapist and the interaction between them. One reason for the focus on the interaction is that it is the only setting in which the therapist can accurately assess discrepancies between the patient's own description of the experience and the experience itself. In other words, if a patient repeatedly describes his wife's callous mistreatment of him, the therapist does not usually have enough data to know if the description is accurate or includes some distortion. However, if the patient harshly criticizes the therapist for his callous treatment of him when the therapist has merely been adhering to his role, then the therapist has a clearer view of the patient's tendency to perceive external real objects through the distorting lens of an internal object representation. Therefore, TFP therapists must be careful to resist the very human temptation to immediately correct a distorted image of themselves because it is precisely this distorted image which brings essential data to the therapy.[1]

The following example illustrates this point. A therapist began a session five minutes after the scheduled time and the patient's first words were:

> It's more and more clear that you don't like me and don't want to see me. Every day there's another sign of it. Your keeping me waiting like that just shows that you wish I would go away, and I almost did. If you had kept me waiting one more minute, I would have been out of there and you wouldn't have seen me again.

---

1. J. Steiner, *Psychic Retreats: Pathological Organization of the Personality in Psychotic, Neurotic, and Borderline Patients* (London: Routledge and The Institute of Psychoanalysis, 1993), pp. 131–146.

Many therapists would be tempted to respond with a combination of defensiveness and reassurance, intending to be supportive of the patient's efforts to change but without getting to the root of the problem:

> It's important to look at your reaction here. You tend to be so rigid and demanding of yourself and others that there's no room for leeway. A five-minute delay is usually within the norms of human behavior. The fact that you turn it into a reason to castigate me and conclude that I don't like you is intimately related to the difficulty you have maintaining a close relation with anybody.

A TFP therapist would rather respond:

> Tell me more about how you see me right now. My opening the door five minutes late was evidence to you that I don't like you. Can you elaborate on how you think I feel about you and what you think the reasons for my not liking you are?

The therapist might later intervene with a comment such as:

> If you are convinced that I don't like you, what is your understanding of why I am seeing you?

In many cases, the patient can achieve some insight on his own as he pursues this elaboration. He may see that his description of the therapist's attitude toward him is so extreme that it begins to "fall from its own weight" like a cantilevered extension of a building that goes out so far it can no longer hold itself up. The patient may see contradictions in his own reporting; he may realize that his extreme negative description of the therapist does not fit with other data available, such as the fact that the previous week the therapist went out of his way to reschedule a session for the patient.

Nevertheless, there are also times when patients are firmly entrenched in their projection and do not achieve any insight on their own. At these times, the therapist must take a more active role. In extreme cases, the patient's perception includes distorting objective facts so that, in the example above, a patient might say:

You kept me waiting for half the session—you might as well just tell me not to come.

A first order of business in a case like this is to see to what degree the patient and therapist share a common view of the facts before exploring the meaning these facts have to the patient. In this situation, the therapist might say:

When you said I kept you waiting half the session time, did you mean that literally, or was that a figure of speech?

If the patient acknowledges he exaggerated for effect, the therapist can go on to explore the patient's view of him and the meaning of the five-minute delay. If, however, the patient says:

You kept me waiting twenty minutes, and if you don't admit it, you're a liar and I'm leaving here right now,

the therapist must confront the patient's discrepant views of reality before proceeding. The therapist might say:

You are saying I opened the door twenty minutes late; I am saying I opened the door five minutes late. We can't both be right. We have to look at the different possibilities here. Both of us can't be right. One of us is wrong, and incapable of reconsidering his position. It's as if a normal person and a madman were in the room, and we can't decide who is who. Therefore, I suggest we agree there's an element of madness in the room and we try to figure out where this madness is coming from. The only other alternative is that one of us is lying. If you think I'm lying, please tell me so we can explore what that would mean.

This method is calling *exploring incompatible realities* and, as is usual in TFP, it includes exploration of the transference. The essential issue is that for the moment the therapist and patient have no common basis in reality. The priority issue is then to clarify the nature of the fantasy involved in this madness. How does the patient understand the incompatible realities? Is the therapist malicious, ignorant, stupid, or crazy? Is the therapist so inattentive or indifferent as to not be able to keep track of the time? Does the therapist devalue the patient to the point that he would lie to him? Can the patient consider the possibility that his perception of events is inaccurate or distorted? If the patient thinks the therapist is lying, why is the therapist lying? Why does the patient come to see a therapist he believes is capable of lying?

In extreme cases, the patient may firmly hold onto a view that represents a temporary loss of reality testing. In these cases the therapist must make the diagnostic distinction between an acute episode of psychosis, which can sometimes occur in the course of treatment with a borderline patient, versus a transference psychosis in which the loss of reality testing occurs only in relation to the therapist and does not affect the patient's life outside the therapy.

A final word on the balance between elaborating the distorted view and establishing common elements of reality is that in most cases the perceptions of borderline patients are based on some element of external reality. This makes it especially important for the therapist to maintain a sense of proportion and to periodically ask himself a very important question:

How does the patient's reaction compare to what an expectable reaction within the normal range would be?

This question is based on a *practical, operational definition of transference*—that transference is any reaction of the patient to the therapist that is beyond what a normal expectable reaction might be. For example, in the case of the therapist starting the session five minutes late, it is true that the therapist kept the patient waiting, but it is also true that a normal expectable response would be for a person to understand that such things happen occasionally without seeing it as "proof" that the therapist disliked that person.

It is important that beginning therapists remember to compare patients' reactions to what a normal expectable reaction would be because the power of patients' intense affects can sometimes convince others that their "reading" of the "grain of truth" is an accurate one and that it has nothing to do with an aspect of their inner world which needs to be analyzed. This power of conviction of the patient's way of perceiving things can be as significant in situations of positive transference as it is at times of negative transference. The classic example of the latter is a situation where the patient reacts to a relatively benign or expectable action of the therapist as though it were severe mistreatment.

For example, a patient reacted to his therapist's need to schedule a number of weeks away over the next few months as a clear case of mistreatment:

> This is totally unprofessional and disrespectful of your patients; in fact, it's active neglect of your patients. No therapist I've ever heard of takes that much time away from his patients. You should have told me this at the beginning [the therapist had discussed management of times away in the contract setting phase]. It shows you don't care about your patients. It's just my luck to get involved with another person who doesn't give a damn about me, who only cares about himself. But this time, I'm going to do something about it; I'm going to report you to the state licensing board. They should review your license if you're going to treat patients this way, and maybe you shouldn't be treating patients at all.

Faced with this onslaught of intense accusations, beginning therapists might wonder if they had scheduled too much time away and if it was not, indeed, unprofessional. If therapists begin to believe in the patient's accusation, they lose the opportunity to explore what the accusation reveals about the object representations that inhabit the patient's internal world.

An example of a patient having an equally extreme reaction within a positive transference is the following:

> *It's not my imagination this time. I know it . . . you are in love with me. You wouldn't have looked at me that way if you weren't . . . that and the fact that I saw you smile when I said I was thinking of leaving my husband. And when you agreed that I have made progress here, I think that's you're way of telling me that we can end this whole business soon and then we'll be free to do what we both want.*

Again, beginning therapists, who may be aware of some feelings of attraction to their patients, may become preoccupied with doubt about whether they did look at the patient with an expression which might have encouraged these fantasies. More seasoned therapists will realize that, even if there was a friendly expression on their face, the patient's reaction is essentially an expression of elements of her internal world.

It is truly in situations like these that the need to distinguish between internal world and external reality is essential. Difficulty in distinguishing between internal reality and external reality, and some patients' ability to convince others that their internal reality "is" the objective reality, can lead to severe practical problems in the treatment of borderline patients, including charges of mistreatment or inappropriate behavior on the part of the therapist.

46. Why is it important to maintain an awareness of analyzing both the positive and negative aspects of the transference?

Some patients tend to keep one side of their internal split representation of the other out of their verbal communication with the therapist. For example, the patient's expressed feelings toward the therapist may be chronically negative, with repeated accusations that the therapist is doing nothing, is indifferent, is withholding, is cold and cruel, or even is sadistically getting pleasure from seeing the patient suffer. The patient may appear to be stuck in this theme, in this manifestation of the internal split. Therapists sometimes cannot see beyond this negative transference. They may not be sure how to address such a negative onslaught and are often tempted to respond in a defensive way ("But I'm here, doing what I can to try to help you. . . ."). It is more important, at such times, to look very carefully at the other channels of communication, to try to help the patient see the other side of the split and to help the patient understand the need for the split. At the very least, a patient's coming to sessions is a sign of some positive feeling. The therapist might say:

> What you say communicates nothing but negative feelings about me, but we should look at the fact that you're coming here. That fact suggests the presence of some other feelings in you. It's hard to imagine you would come here if what you say again and again represents the entirety of what you feel. It may be that you have no conscious awareness of those feelings, but your coming here may be a sign of a hope, a wish, something that is not clear now, but that is different from what you say.

In some cases, there is more evidence of a split-off positive side than the simple fact of the patient's attendance. The nonverbal communication of the positive transference could, for example, be in the form of the appearance of a smile or a change from a rigid to a relaxed body posture. Therapists should also, of course, monitor their countertransference. One therapist whose patient was entrenched in a negative transference recalled that after the first sessions he had feared the development of a strong positive transference because the patient "was like a young deer, expectantly looking up to me with great deer-like brown eyes." The therapist reflected on the possibility that his reaction represented a concordant countertransference (see discussion of countertransference. Part IV-B question 40) in that early phase of therapy, and used that awareness to suggest to the patient:

> You relentlessly attack me here. It may be that you, in fact, find nothing good about me. However, another possibility is that the hope and wish and longing for something good here is so scary to you that you retreat from it into this negative stance. If that is the case, then we must try to understand why the possibility of something positive is so scary for you.

In some cases, it is the positive transference that seems to become stuck in place with no direct expression of negative transference. The patient's defenses may be organized to try to protect the therapist from the aggression associated with the negative transference. Such patients may come across as very respectful and appreciative of the therapist's efforts. This may especially be the case when the patient experiences the therapist as overtly supportive and fears that any expression of negative sentiment would lead to the loss of that support. The problem is that the patient's appreciativeness of the therapist is not accompanied by any corresponding improvement in life. This lack of improvement in life may be the indirect means by which the patient is expressing the negative dyad of the person who is neglected and deprived. The therapist might say:

> You tell me repeatedly that you are very grateful to be here in therapy with me and that I'm the only therapist you've had who knows what she's doing. However, we have to look at the

whole picture. Your life is not improving. Your relationships continue to be as chaotic as ever and you are on the verge of getting fired at work. This does not exactly fit with the picture of how helpful I am as a therapist and may even be an indirect way of communicating other feelings you may have about me. For instance, you may feel on some level that I am not so helpful and your doing poorly in your life may be a nonverbal protest, a way of saying, "Look at this therapist who says that she's helping me but who's letting my life go down the drain."

Another way in which patients may express the side of the transference that is not being expressed directly in the therapy is through discussion of other important figures in their life. In one case of a relentlessly negative transference, the patient spoke repeatedly of her "crush" on a co-worker. When talking about him, her affect changed to one of girlish coquettishness. When the therapist felt confidant enough that the patient's expressions of affection and longing were also (and perhaps primarily) connected to him, he proposed this possibility to the patient:

> While you say you have nothing but negative feelings for me, your insistence on telling me all the time about your crush on John and the feelings you seem to experience as you tell me that somehow suggest that you may be experiencing feelings toward me which are quite the contrary of what you express. It would be important for us to explore this possibility and to understand why it is so difficult for you to have any conscious awareness of these feelings.

As is always the case with TFP, the work is a balance between exploring the current transference and exploring what it may be defending against. An example of a therapist attempting to further explore the nature of an apparently all positive, idealized transference is as follows:

> You keep telling me how your wife fails you, your boss disappoints you and your parents are never there for you. Yet

you say I'm the perfect therapist for you and you even wish
we could run off together because you're sure you'd find the
happiness with me that no one else can provide you. It would
be interesting to understand better what sets me apart from
all these others in your mind and what you think I have
which would lead to perfect satisfaction instead of the
universal disappointment you report with others.

It is important to note in this discussion that transference is
not always divided neatly into positive and negative. Love and
aggression can be closely entangled in a patient's presentation. For
example, a patient who professed her strong love for her therapist
urged him to give up the "artificial constraints" of being a therapist
and let himself experience the supreme pleasure she could offer
him. She repeatedly promised that "no one would know" and that
it could only be a good experience for both of them. What at first
glance seems to be an expression of love is an attack on the
relationship, a threat to destroy the therapy and an invitation for
the therapist to join in a joint betrayal. This is an example of how
aggression can be disguised as seduction. How this situation might
be interpreted can be seen in example 3a of question 41 (p. 145).
The reverse can be true when the angry, petulant patient is hoping
to be understood and loved.

Part V

TREATMENT TECHNIQUES

47. What are the techniques used in TFP?

They are:

1. The *interpretive process*, including *clarification, confrontation,* and *interpretation* per se. It may be helpful for the therapist to consider clarification and confrontation as steps that prepare the way for interpretation, which is considered the most important tool for bringing about intrapsychic integration and, thereby, change in personality structure.
2. *Transference analysis* directed at a systematic analysis of primitive defenses as they enter the transference (this technique is important in the long-term strengthening of the ego in that it brings back to the patient what he is projecting or denying, but it can be difficult in the short term because of the patient's anxiety in "taking back" what he is projecting).[1]
3. Appropriate *management of technical neutrality*
4. An ongoing *integration of countertransference data* into the interpretive process

---

1. It is precisely this technique, which is at the core of TFP, which leads some critics of this method to criticize it as harsh since much of what is projected and must be "taken back" has to do with split-off aggression. At issue is the role of aggression in the patient's psyche. While no one would argue that many borderline patients have been subjected to terrible aggression in the course of their development, a psychoanalytic understanding of the human condition views aggression as a constituent part of every individual and assumes that an individual is better adjusted if he is aware of and in control of aggression that, if left unconscious, would become manifest in acting out or symptoms. Some therapies, however, focus on aggression only insofar as the patient has been victim of it. These therapies do not endorse the idea of the patient having his own aggression as a constituent part of his psyche.

48. What is meant by clarification in TFP?

Clarification is the therapist's invitation to the patient to explain and explore any information that is unclear, vague, puzzling, or contradictory. It is not the therapist's providing clarification to the patient, but is rather *the therapist's seeking clarification from the patient*. It may focus on any material the patient brings up such as elements of external reality, the patient's past, or the patient's current feelings and fantasies, including, of course, those about the therapist. Clarification serves both the purpose of elucidating specific information and of discovering the extent to which the patient seems to have a clear understanding of the material or is confused by it.

The process of clarification helps the patient bring out new elements of the selected communication, which may throw light on previously obscure or unknown aspects. In its most basic form, clarification simply allows the therapist to understand the surface level of what the patient is saying. Beginning therapists sometimes hesitate to seek clarification as much as is necessary, given the usual state of confusion within the patient's internal world. This hesitation can correspond to the implicit expectation of the patient that the therapist should be the perfect, omniscient caregiver. If the therapist fails to understand everything immediately and needs to ask questions, the patient may respond by harshly devaluing the therapist for not meeting this primitive expectation of being the perfect provider. The therapist is better off understanding that this hesitation is based on the projection of this primitive object than trying to avoid a devaluing response by pretending to understand when this is not possible.

Examples of a therapist seeking clarification are:

> —You just referred to dropping out of college. I don't believe you ever mentioned being in college. Could you tell me something about that part of your life.
> —It's not clear to me who the person you've been referring to as "Suzy" is.

—You said your experience growing up was "pretty normal." Could you explain to me what you mean by that?

—You said that I was treating you just like your father. Could you elaborate on what you mean by that?

49. What is meant by confrontation in TFP?

Confrontation is the technique that points to evidence that the patient's communication includes material that is split-off and un-integrated in the patient's psyche. The aim of confrontation is to make the patient aware of incongruous aspects of the material being communicated. Confrontation brings together material, whether it be unconscious, preconscious, or conscious, which the patient experiences separately, or does not experience but acts out (or somatizes). This technique consists of drawing the patient's attention to contradictions in the patient's material that either has been outside the patient's awareness or has been assumed to be perfectly natural even though it is discrepant with other ideas, feelings or actions of the patient. In making confrontations, the therapist may either refer to material that has been communicated at different times through the same channel (e.g., verbal) but which is in contradiction, or may refer to discrepancies in what is being communicated through the different channels, sometimes simultaneously.

It is important to note that confrontation is carried out with courtesy and tact. It is not done with the belligerent quality that can be a connotation of the term confrontation. Simply put, it is not a hostile confrontation; it is rather a curious confrontation in which the therapist genuinely wants to know the patient's thinking about how element X and element Y of his communication fit, or do not fit, together. Nevertheless, even when a confrontation is communicated with adequate tact, it might be experienced by the patient as hostile since the technique highlights and questions the patient's defensive system of splitting.

Examples of confrontation are:

> —The last time you were here, you were telling me how much smarter you are than anyone else at your job. Today, you are saying that you made an unforgivable mistake and you're convinced you're going to be fired. If you stop for a minute to look at these two messages, what are your thoughts? How do you put them together?

—You've been telling me, in no uncertain terms, how stupid and useless you think I am. Yet even as you're saying this, you have what looks like an engaging smile and a twinkle in your eye. Do you have any thoughts about that?

—You keep saying it's a waste of time for you to come here, but today when I said I would be away for a week next month, you looked very upset and asked if we could make up the sessions we'll be missing. On the surface, this seems like a contradiction. Do you have any thoughts about it?

—You tell me you've given up on everyone and that if you can't "get your act together" enough to live totally independently from the rest of the world, you're going to kill yourself. You're telling me this in a defiant way and suggesting that I'll never see you again. And yet, there's a subtle look in your eyes that seems to want to connect with me, that seems to be entreating me to not give up on you. I think we have to look at both aspects of your communication. What do you think?

As stated above, both clarification and confrontation can be thought of as preparing the way for interpretation. In some instances, confrontation allows patients to do some of the interpretive work themselves. In the last of the examples above, a patient might respond by saying:

It's hard to look at this, but I think you're right. I'm beginning to see that the closer I feel to someone, the more I retreat into that kind of isolation . . . the more I push them away. I guess it doesn't make sense. But it does make sense . . . it does make sense because I know that everyone will eventually dump me. That's why I feel so uncomfortable when I feel close . . . I know it won't work out. I guess I don't really want to live totally separate from everybody. I guess I want to be close, but it seems impossible.

50. What is meant by interpretation?

Most generally, interpretations are attempts to understand the workings of the individual's psyche by gaining insight into the impact of unconscious material on the patient's thoughts, feelings, and actions. More specifically, interpretations address the question of why a particular conflict exists in the individual's psyche with the idea that an understanding of the reason for the conflict will help the patient resolve it. Since the psychological structure of borderline patients is characterized by split-off, unintegrated self-other dyads which carry drives and prohibitions, interpretations in these cases address the reasons why the fragmented, split intra-psychic structure is maintained—the *motivation* for the ongoing internal fragmentation.

Interpretations utilize information from clarification and confrontation, with careful attention to all three channels of communication, to link material the patient is conscious of with inferred, hypothesized unconscious material believed to be influencing the patient's understanding [way of perceiving], affects, motivation and functioning. The therapist first brings to the patient's awareness aspects of the patient's internal experience of which the patient seems not to be consciously aware. The therapist then proposes hypotheses about why this material is kept out of the patient's awareness. The process assumes that the patient's understanding of unconscious conflicts between the unintegrated parts of the patient's internal world will make apparent contradictions logical, and maladaptive behaviors understandable.

In TFP, the therapist tends to focus on interpretations of the transference in the here-and-now. Nevertheless, interpretations may also address the patient's current external reality, past external reality, or characteristic defenses. In addition, the therapist may link any of these elements with the assumed unconscious past (genetic interpretations).

51. What are the different levels of interpretation?

The therapist may address different levels of the patient's psychological functioning. The therapist may:

1. Interpret how acting out or primitive defenses are serving to avoid awareness of internal experience;
2. Interpret the object relations dyad which is currently active, describing the self and object representations in the dyad and any role reversals observed; or
3. Interpret the object relation dyad which the currently active dyad appears to be defending against.

The therapist is generally advised to interpret from the first level to the third since the patient's defenses are usually more immediately observable—both closer to the "surface" of the material and also closer to the patient's awareness than the material (impulses and conflicts) which is being defended against. This is referred to as *interpreting from surface to depth.* It is important to note that the levels of interpretation are not mutually exclusive—both because defenses are often expressed through object relations dyads and because conflicts, impulses, and defenses are interconnected.

Examples of the levels are as follows:

1a) **This is the second time that you have called up your old boyfriend when I was away for a week. You've said that it's always a disaster to have any contact with him, that he's totally unreliable and "sweet talks" you with false promises. It seems this behavior is a way to try to avoid feeling something when I go away. Whatever you're trying to do by contacting him at these times doesn't seem to work since, in any case, you're left feeling terrible. It would be best for us to try to understand more fully what goes on in you when I go away so you don't keep repeating this behavior pattern which leaves you feeling bad over and over again.** [Interpreting acting out as avoiding awareness of internal experience.]

It is likely that the awareness being avoided in this example is not simply feeling abandoned by the therapist, but is the awareness of anger toward the therapist because of the "abandonment." Since the patient's behavior in response to the therapist's leaving is harmful to her, the implicit message is an accusation that the therapist is hurting her.

> 1b) **It seems as though every time I suggest you seem angry here, you give me another example of your husband losing his temper and making you feel afraid and at risk. While it's not for me to question that your husband has angry outbursts, you seem distinctly uncomfortable with the notion that you might feel anger. Meanwhile, you ended the last session here by storming out of the office and slamming the door** [bringing it into the transference]. **Another relevant piece of the picture is that you sometimes ask me "out of the blue" if I'm angry. Putting these things together makes me wonder if you do, indeed, experience anger, but that it is so distasteful to you that you do not experience it as such but perceive it, perhaps sometimes accurately and sometimes not, in other people.** [Interpreting projection]

> 2a) **While you're not explicitly saying it, your manner toward me—you're anxiously justifying every decision you make with a demeanor that could almost be described as cowering— suggests you're afraid of me, as though I were an angry, arbitrary tyrant who could punish you at the drop of a hat and you are a helpless, defenseless subject at the mercy of my tyranny.** [Interpreting a currently active object representation].

It should be noted that many beginning TFP therapists get to this level of interpretation but have a hard time advancing to the third level where "the reason" for experiencing this dyad is explored.

> 2b) **You've been stating more and more loudly and angrily that you feel I mistreated you by not telling you earlier that**

I'll be away for a week in June. You're saying that I have no respect for you and that I'm a "worthless quack" who treats you "like shit" and who deserves to have his medical license revoked. All the while you seem to experience yourself as a helpless, but noble, victim of my mistreatment. It might be worth taking a minute to reflect what is going on right now in this office. Your loud, angry voice and insulting remarks suggest that you are capable of angry, abusive treatment, but that you do not seem to have any awareness of that. [Interpreting a reversal of roles within the dyad.]

3a) You're saying you love me and that you know we'd be perfectly happy together if we just left our spouses and ran off together suggests that you have nothing but positive feelings for me, extreme positive feelings. However, you know that a therapist's getting involved with a patient is an extreme breech of trust and a betrayal of the patient. It is also the one thing a therapist could do which would be most destructive to his career. So we've got to look further here. I don't doubt that you may have strong positive, even loving feelings, for me. But the way you express them suggests that there are also feelings that are very destructive, destructive to this therapeutic relationship, destructive to you, and destructive to me. It may be that the intense love you tell me you feel is attempting to keep other, opposite feelings at bay. Because you *do* like me, it may be very hard for you to deal with, acknowledge, experience the feelings of envy and competitiveness you also feel toward me. Nevertheless, these feelings are suggested in a subtle way by the very form you choose to express your love for me. [Interpreting the dyad which the currently active dyad appears to be defending against and providing a motivation for the need to defend—that the envious and competitive feelings cannot co-exist in the patient's consciousness with the positive, loving feelings.]

3b) A pattern has been emerging in your behavior over the last few weeks. There were some times when a good feeling developed in the course of the session—a feeling of a positive connection between you and me. I noticed that each time there had been that kind of a feeling in a session, you came into the next session very angry and defiant, saying that the therapy was useless, that I was a quack and that you had decided to end the treatment. The interesting, and important, question is: what is the connection between these two states of mind? My sense of what happens is that when you experience the moments of positive contact here, you get in touch with a part of you that is very scary to you—a part of you that wants very much to trust someone and to look to someone—me, at those moments—for help. At those moments, you do not show your usual angry feelings, but seem to demonstrate a tentative, nervous yearning for a sincere connection, like the relation with a caring parent. Then you come in to the next session with the angry defiance. My guess is that the feeling of a positive connection makes you very nervous, and then you retreat into the defiant stance. Why you get so nervous when you feel a positive connection is a very important question that we have to try to understand. It seems as though it feels like a very dangerous place for you to be, as though it couldn't last, or couldn't be real—the "ice will cave in." So you retreat to what you see as the safety of angry defiance. I think it's very important that we now see this anger is not the whole picture, that underneath that side of you there is a side that is yearning for a positive connection. [Interpreting how the aggressively-charged dyad is defending against the libidinally-charged dyad. This example also illustrates how the therapist must sometimes consider the pattern of the patient's behavior over a number of sessions in order to have all the data necessary for an interpretation.]

3c) You've been telling me since the beginning of this session that you have given up on therapy. You say that I've turned out to be just like everyone else in your life—at first you think I'm on your side and you can trust me, and then you decide that I'm selfish and only interested in what I can get out of you. So your plan is to leave everything—your husband, your children, your home—and to move to some remote place and "try to make it on your own." You say you're aware how unlikely it is that you'll be able to succeed, so you see your plan as likely to end with your suicide. You say you feel comfortable with this plan because it is the "only thing that makes sense in a world where you can't trust anyone." I agree that there is a certain internal logic to your thinking— but only if your thinking includes the whole picture, and I don't think it does. The reason I don't think it does is because of the look in your eye. There is a subtle look in your eye that is imploring me to help you. It is the look of someone who is being held captive and is terrified to speak up. I think in a way you are being held captive; you're being held captive by a part of you that trusts no one, that sees everyone as selfish and exploiting, that feels you can only be the object that others use and take advantage of. Yet in the look in your eyes, there is the expression of another side of you that feels and hopes that there can be a genuine, authentic, caring connection with someone else. But it seems this possibility is so fraught with fear—the fear that it is wrong and that you will be left used and hurt again—that the more cynical side of you is trying to silence it. Ironically, the side of you that is choosing a likely death seems safer to you than the side of you that believes an honest relation with another person can exist. We have to look more at why you seem to fear a relationship more than death itself.

52. How should interpretations be delivered?

When therapists feel they have enough data from the patient's words and behaviors, as well as, from their own countertransference, they should spell out their interpretations in detail and with conviction. Even though the interpretation is an hypothesis, it is best to deliver it with conviction both because it is based on careful analysis of available data and because the patient may respond with resistance even if it is correct. In our discussion of defenses, we emphasized how patients have difficulty accepting a part of their internal reality that they deny and/or project. It may help to introduce an interpretation with a statement that empathizes with the patient's split internal world. For example, if the therapist is about to comment on a part of the patient's internal world which is split-off (e.g., aggression), the therapist might say:

> I'm aware you could hear what I am about to say as a criticism or possibly an insult, but if you do, consider the possibility that the disapproval you sense might be coming from within you.

While interpretation is largely the communication of an idea, like any form of communication, the delivery has a great deal to do with how effective it is. Therefore, the skilled therapist must be aware of the issues of *relevance, clarity, depth, and speed of interpretation*. Is the interpretation *relevant* in that it is addressing a conflict that is affectively dominant at the present moment? Is the interpretation *clearly stated*? Interventions are best made in simple and clear language, both to avoid the sterility of intellectual-sounding interventions and to attempt to connect with both the patient's affects as well as mind.

Is the *speed* of the therapist's intervention appropriate? If the therapist intervenes too quickly, "on a hunch," the therapist may not be able to point to enough data in the material to make a convincing case for the hypothesis. Alternatively, the patient may find the quick intervention evidence that the therapist has the wished-for omniscience of the perfect provider. If the therapist waits too long to intervene, the therapeutic dialogue becomes lifeless. Beginning therapists may hesitate to propose an idea until they feel absolutely sure of it. Their hesitation is often a response to the fragmentation of the interaction with the patient, a discontinuity caused by rapid shifts from one dyad to another or reversals of the self/object poles within a dyad. Therapists are advised in such circumstances to name the dyad they are experiencing as soon as they can. Trying to wait until the whole picture becomes clear often leads to getting lost in a rapidly changing presentation.

Is the interpretation at the *appropriate depth*? Under normal circumstances, interpretations proceed "from surface to depth,"[2] including first a description of the defensive level and then an interpretation of what is being defended against. Beginning therapists often do not include the latter. A classic example is the therapist who says:

You're experiencing me as a detached scientist who treats you like a guinea pig in an experiment without adding

---

2. An exception to this rule is that, in extreme conditions when the therapy is in jeopardy (e.g., if the patient seems on the verge of dropping out), the therapist may have to proceed immediately to a deep interpretation without having the chance to work from surface to depth. For example, "You say you won't be coming back here because it's a waste of your time, and you seem very firm about that and at peace with the decision. Even though there isn't a clear sign of it in your attitude or behavior right now. I have reason to believe that your decision to leave therapy right now might be because you have begun to feel better in some way and that it is hard for you to tolerate that feeling. It may be that the possibility that I can help you sets off a reaction in you where you feel inferior and humiliated. Then, you attack the source of the humiliation—the therapy that is the very thing that could help you. I think it's very important you consider this possibility before acting on your impulse to leave therapy." The therapist bases this interpretation on the understanding of the patient's narcissistic dynamics. If the patient were not on the verge of leaving therapy, the therapist might wait to have more evidence of the patient's feeling humiliated before making this interpretation.

> You may insist on seeing our interaction in this way because
> of the anxiety you feel at any moment when you experience
> me in a more human way. When that happens, a moment of
> positive connection seems to be followed by the automatic
> fear that any genuine interest I might appear to have in you is
> just a set-up for a cruel rejection and abandonment to follow.

Finally, there has to be an internal consistency in the therapist's approach to the patient. Keeping the structural principle (Part IV-B, question 39) in mind can be helpful here. While being attentive to the interaction in the moment, the therapist should keep in mind the "background," that is, the most fundamental conflicts or chronic baseline transference issues. For example, when a patient complains in session "I'm bored, I shouldn't have come today," the therapist's first response is to explore the boredom. However, if the patient goes no further than to repeat that she is "bored, just bored—don't you get it?," the therapist should base an intervention of the understanding of the basic underlying issues in the current phase of therapy and link the current moment to those issues. For example:

> Your boredom may appear to be unconnected to anything we
> have been discussing in the past sessions. However, although
> it may appear to be separate from the intense rage you were
> expressing last week about my going away, it could just be
> the flip side of the coin. It could be a manifestation of your
> rage attacking and destroying any feeling of connection to
> me, or any sense of meaning to our work together. Nothing is
> left but boredom, but behind that is the rage of feeling, once
> again in your life, seduced and abandoned.

53. How does the therapist go about the transference analysis of primitive defenses?

As was discussed in Part I, question 7, there is an intimate relation between primitive defense mechanisms and object relations dyads. The primitive defenses serve to maintain the basic split structure of the psyche. Since this split structure serves the purpose of protecting the patient from anxiety in a very rudimentary way, the therapist must be aware that efforts to interpret these defenses to the patient will be met with resistance. This is because *the patient is invested in maintaining the split that spares the patient the pain of internal conflict by externalizing or denying one side of the internal split.* It is this investment in the split structure which leads many patients to seek a response from the therapist which reinforces the split as in the case of patients who attempt to deny and externalize their aggressive part and ask the therapist to accept the view that their role is solely that of the victim and that all aggression comes from outside. As a result, the therapist must work with empathy and understand that analyzing the primitive defense mechanisms can create distress in the patient even though it is necessary to do this in order to achieve the integrated internal structure which will allow the patient to experience a full range of affect and to engage in life more successfully and on a deeper level.

Splitting. The therapist's awareness of splitting comes from observing the patient's tendency to describe self and others in extreme terms and also to abruptly shift descriptions of the self and others from one extreme to the other. The therapist's attention to splitting should always include thinking about the question:

> **Why must the patient do this . . . what purpose does it serve?**

It is in helping the patient understand the reason for the splitting that the therapist will help the patient move beyond the need to function at that primitive level.

For example, a patient repeatedly shifted from an idealized positive view of the therapist to a totally devalued negative one. The therapist proposed the following understanding to the patient:

> Every time you perceive something in me that disappoints you, even if it is only a few minutes delay in starting the session, you switch from an extremely positive view of me to saying that I am worthless and useless and that it is a waste of your time to come here. I don't doubt that you experience each view sincerely at the time you are feeling it, but it might help to understand why it is that your view can shift so radically. Your positive view of me—that I am perfectly wise and educated and the only therapist who could understand you—is so extreme that it represents a need for you to believe there is someone in the world who can respond ideally, flawlessly to your needs. Whenever there is a suggestion, as there repeatedly is, that I cannot care for you perfectly, you reject me radically as worthless. This inability to accept any imperfection or limitation in me may be your way of holding on to an image you cherish dearly, that of the perfect provider. However, your response to my imperfections is to dismiss me totally, leaving you alone with no help at all. It may be that the greatest threat to your having someone to care about you in the world is not my, or another's imperfections, but the aggression with which you attack anyone in your life who does not meet your perfect image/expectation. In that sense, the ideal view you hold onto as your salvation may actually be part of a system of thinking and reacting which leads to your increasing isolation.

The above example reminds us that *idealization/devaluation* is a form of *splitting.*

In another example, a patient repeatedly attacked her therapist for only being interested in her for the income she provided and accused him of keeping her ill to drain her of all her money. The patient's history included a series of relationships with wealthy men who supported her financially. The patient could not tolerate her awareness of her own exploitative side and projected it onto her therapist.

Projection. As the above example suggests, splitting is often expressed as projection. A common projection in therapy with borderline patients is that of the harsh, critical, condemning voice. It might happen that every time the therapist seeks clarification about something the patient has said, the patient responds as though the inquiry is a criticism and a condemnation, saying:

> *I can't say anything without you getting on my case for it. You're wondering why I missed my job interview . . . I just missed it! Don't you get it? And here you are blaming me for it.*

It is often difficult for a patient to accept that the harsh critical judge is a part of the patient's own internal world even though there may be ample evidence for it in frequent harsh critiques of self and others.

Projective identification. In this form of projection, the patient induces an affect in the therapist that the patient is uncomfortable experiencing and integrating in himself. Monitoring this defense requires the therapist to be acutely aware of countertransference. A part of this technique is for therapists to be aware of any internal response they are having in a session that deviates from their usual range of responses. For example, a therapist was sitting with a patient who had a history of violent suicide attempts, but who, between the attempts, presented as very controlled and mild-mannered. During the first months of therapy, the patient was very well-behaved, but the therapist felt she had little to work with and was worried that the patient's history of sudden brutal suicide attempts would repeat itself. In a session when the therapist had announced an upcoming absence, the patient began to devalue the therapist in a cold, detached way. Without any visible affect, the patient made comments such as:

> *It's interesting you bring up that you're going to be away. Before you said that, I was going to tell you that I was thinking about how useless it is to come here. I've been feeling this way since about our second session together, but I've put off telling you that because it's hard for*

me to hurt anyone's feelings. But I finally decided I can't sacrifice my time and money any more just to spare your feelings. It's worthless coming here and it's better to say it and move on. To sit here and pretend you're a good therapist would be like ignoring an elephant in the room.

The therapist attempted to link the patient's devaluing of her to angry feelings about her taking some time away. The patient calmly dismissed the idea that there was any connection and continued with his devaluing comments. After forty minutes of this, the therapist began to notice violent fantasies spontaneously emerging in her, such as an image of strangling the patient. As soon as she reflected on this, she realized that this was not in the range of her usual responses to patients and that it was therefore likely that the emergence of these fantasies was provoked by the patient's use of projective identification. She became aware of the hatred in the fantasies and realized that her remarks about the patient's likely anger toward her were mild in comparison to the wish to destroy her that he was splitting-off and projecting onto her. This awareness allowed her to make interventions with more conviction and with more specificity; she spoke of the "hatred" and the "wish to destroy" rather than anger. Although the patient did not immediately agree with her interventions, their dialogue moved out of the impasse it had been in. The patient could eventually acknowledge his hatred, which he later said he could not previously admit to because he feared it would actually destroy anyone it came in touch with. His attempt to deny such a central affect in his internal world had left him in the bland emotional paralysis that had characterized the first months of therapy.

One aspect of projective identification is that the patient can feel some measure of control over the affect induced in the therapist. In this sense, projective identification has an element of *omnipotent control*, a defense mechanism that can also be observed in other ways in the session.

One common form of omnipotent control found in patients with strong narcissistic features is a tendency to monopolize the dialogue with the therapist. While it is true that patients are instructed to say what comes to mind, some patients speak continuously with a driven quality and talk over the therapist when the therapist attempts to intervene. In this situation, the patient's style of speech communicates more important information than the content of what the patient is saying. It would be pointless for the therapist to try to pick up on any particular theme in the patient's discourse because the most important information is in the patient's interaction with the therapist. Therefore, the therapist must address the patient's way of speaking, with the usual question in mind of why it is important that the patient act in this way. The therapist might say:

> I am going to have to interrupt you. Are you interested in what I am going to say? [The therapist must say this firmly because the patient generally goes on talking. When the patient has stopped the therapist continues.] It's important to look at your way of speaking to me. You go on and on, changing topics without stopping, not letting me speak when I try. There is something about this that it would be important to understand. Two ideas come to my mind, and there may be other ways to understand it as well. The first idea is that your way of speaking controls the situation here and controls me. That seems clear. It would be important to try to understand why you need to do that . . . what you expect or fear would happen if you did not do that. Perhaps you fear that if you do not constantly control our interaction that I would either turn away from you or attack you in some way [Tentatively identifying one dyad]. This is not all clear, but we should explore these possibilities. The second idea is that you seem to be feeding me an endless stream of information. Perhaps you have the idea that if you just give me enough information, I will have power to heal you, to fix what is wrong in you. [Identifying a second possible dyad]

54. What is technical neutrality and how does the therapist manage it in TFP?

First, it is important to emphasize that technical neutrality is *not* the bland, monotonous, indifferent tone suggested by some caricatures of analytic therapists. It is rather the therapist's avoiding taking sides when discussing and exploring the patient's conflicts. Psychological conflicts are understood as involving competing forces from the id, the ego, the superego, and external reality. Technical neutrality refers to the therapist's helping the patient observe and understand all the forces active in a conflict so that the patient can make as fully informed a decision as possible. For example, a patient's statement:

> *I met this guy at a bar last night and he's so sexy I think I'll leave my husband and run off with him, but I don't know. . . .*

suggests a conflict between libidinal id forces (sexual desire), superego forces (rules and values), ego forces (judgment), and external reality (what would the overall impact on the patient's life be?). The TFP therapist avoids taking sides in such a conflict for three reasons. First, if the therapist were to take a side, it would counter the overall goal of the patient's growth in understanding and autonomy. Second, after some exploration, the interplay of forces might not be what it seems on the surface (e.g., perhaps the impulse to "run off" is not determined so much by libidinal forces as by punitive superego forces in that running off would probably lead to difficult complications in the patient's life that could serve the purpose of punishing her for her libidinal impulses). Third, the TFP point of view always includes understanding the meaning of the patient's interaction with the therapist—is the patient in this situation trying to force the therapist to act on her behalf? If so, why?

The therapist might have to address each of these points, starting with the transference:

> The way you present this situation to me suggests you are on
> the verge of taking impulsive action. We both know that
> impulsive actions have been a major source of difficulties in
> your life. So the situation you are describing includes your
> coming in and telling me about it in this way. The way you
> are telling me this comes across as an appeal for me to
> intervene, to get involved. I think we have to examine that
> wish as we consider this situation you are bringing to this
> session. . . .

In addition to exploring the transference aspects of the situation, the exploration of the situation itself might lead to a fuller understanding of the configuration of intrapsychic forces represented in the situation. For example, as suggested above, it might be that the apparent id force (going for the sexy guy) actually represented a punitive superego force that would punish her for her sexual urges. The possibility of exploring this situation in full would be limited if therapist jumped into the situation by taking a side.

In spite of the general rule that the therapist maintain technical neutrality, the therapist may have to deviate from this rule in certain situations which arise with borderline patients. This is the case when the patient is on the verge of acting in an impulsive way that would be directly harmful to the patient or the therapy. If in the above example, the patient had stated:

> *I met this sexy guy at a bar and it was so exciting . . . I couldn't
> believe it, I've never felt that way before. I just know if I spend my life
> with him, I'll be OK. We've decided to run off together tonight. I'll
> just tell my husband I'm going out to the drugstore to pick up my
> medication.*

Since the therapist's ability to work with the patient requires that they meet and have the time to explore the material, the patient's stated plan is immediately threatening to the therapy in two ways. First, the patient is currently financially dependent on her husband so that leaving him would leave her without the means to pay for therapy (perhaps part of a test to see if her therapist "really loves her" and would see her for nothing), and second, her plan is to take off for "parts unknown" with the man from the bar, taking her away from therapy. In this situation, the therapist is obliged to side with what is available in the patient's rational, observing ego.

The therapist might say:

> You know, I don't usually take a role in your decisions, but what you are saying now is such a threat to our work together that I have to express an opinion. While it's not for me to decide what you do with your life, and I can't pretend to know what is best in a situation we have not yet had the time to explore, I must state very strongly that I think it would be a big mistake for you to take any action right now because the full meaning and implications of the situation are not clear and your plan robs us of the possibility of working toward an understanding of it. So I must urge you do hold off on your plan to run off with this man until we have the time to explore it. I don't usually take this firm a position, but you are forcing me to do so by telling me you are about to abruptly end your therapy because you feel a man you just met is the guarantee of future happiness.

Any time the therapist abandons neutrality, the therapist must then, in the course of analyzing the situation, explore the meaning of the patient's having forced the therapist to do so. In other words, the analysis of the situation includes understanding the transference implications of it. In the above example, the therapist might at some point say:

> It is interesting that while you described the man from the bar as the key to your future happiness, you put me in a position of having to "save" you from what you now see as a very dangerous situation. It is as if you were placing me in a situation where if I did not act as your "hero" to save you,

then I would have come across as an indifferent bystander who would sit back and let you jump off the cliff, so to speak. Could it be that in your mind, if a person isn't actively engaged in saving you, you experience them as indifferent?

55. How do therapists monitor their countertransference and integrate what they learn from it into the treatment?

The general principle is that therapists monitor their reactions to patients for any reaction that deviates from their usual responses. This is parallel to monitoring patients for any response that is not within a usual, expectable range. What complicates this process is that the therapist's reaction may be provoked either by something in the patient or by something in the therapist's own psyche. For example, if a patient describes an aggressive fantasy and the therapist experiences a feeling of fear, the therapist's reaction could represent:

1. A concordant countertransference (an identification with the patient's current self-representation which gives the therapist a sense of the patient's current subjective state),
2. A complementary countertransference (an identification with a projected split offs object-representation, which gives the therapists a sense of a state within the patient that is split-off), or
3. The activation of a conflict or issue within the therapist's psyche.

As discussed in Part IV-B, question 40, therapists must be able to analyze and understand the source of their countertransference. The task is not always easy and may take some time of reflection. It is important that therapists have had the opportunity to explore their own internal world in a personal experience of therapy. It is also important that a TFP therapist be at ease with primary process material, that is, with the kind of primitive feelings related to basic drives and affects that emerge in fantasies, dreams, and acting out behaviors (see Part IX, question 74 regarding primary process material).

At times, discussing a case in individual or group supervision may help therapists sort out what part of their reaction is provoked by the patient and what may be coming from the therapist.

Part VI

COURSE OF TREATMENT
AFTER THE CONTRACT

56. What are the phases of TFP?

TFP can be described from the logical sequential analysis of beginning, middle, and end of treatment. The beginning of treatment involves assessment and setting of the treatment contract. We have described assessment earlier in terms of the structural interview leading to a structural diagnosis of the patient, and taking of clinical history. We have also described the importance and process of setting the treatment contract that specifies the responsibilities and obligations of both therapist and patient, and obtains the patient's agreement to the conditions of the treatment. The middle of treatment is the repetitive analysis of the dominant object relations that are manifested in the here-and-now interaction of the sessions. The ending of the treatment is a mutually agreed upon bringing to a close of the relationship that was examined in detail.

From the perspective of the dominant transference, it is typical that patients progress from a paranoid transference and psychological organization to a depressive transference and psychological organization. This has been described above in Part II, question 17.

From the point of view of the individual patient, the phases of treatment vary in duration and content. This is because patients who are at a borderline level of organization vary in terms of interpersonal relatedness, presence versus absence of any internalized values, and pervasiveness of aggression. The more disturbed, low level borderline patients with more infusion of aggression into their self-experience and relationships are more difficult to engage in a therapeutic alliance, and have more need for major change in a number of areas. Given that the goal of TFP is change in the organization of the personality, this task will in general take longer and be slower for patients with BPO who have a more pervasive infusion of aggression in their lives and a poorer initial capacity for relating to others.

57. Does treatment generally demonstrate a linear progression?

No, the general progression includes a mix of advances "plateaus," and regressions. In the midst of these periods, the treatment may be punctuated at any time, especially in the early phases, by *affect storms* (see Part VI, question 61). During plateau periods, the therapist should focus on the basic work of understanding the principle dyads in the patient's internal world and how they are in conflict. Advances may be apparent either in the manifestation of a new aspect of the patient's internal world or in the patient's demonstrating an understanding of the relation between different parts of his or her internal world. An example of both types of advance, and also of regression, can be seen in the case discussed below (Part VII, question 64A) where the patient denied for the first months of treatment that she had any feelings toward the therapist except the wish to use his skills to stop feeling bad and acting out so that she could live independently of and separate from everyone else. The first advance in this case was the dramatic emergence of the very dependent and attached part of the patient when the therapist announced that he would be away a second time: her "You can't go!" reaction. Of course, even after that moment, the patient shifted regularly to the opposite—"I don't need or want you or anyone else"—side of the split, even to the point that, when her therapist confronted her with the contradiction between the two sides, she sometimes denied that she had ever said that she did not want him to go away. The second advance on this theme came after a number of months when the therapist had repeated on many occasions the interpretation that the patient professed her strong wish for total independence because of the anxiety and pain she experienced whenever she became aware of her great longing to be close to someone. The patient said:

> *I guess you're right. It does seem that every time I feel a closeness, even for a minute, I get terrified and fight it.*

This statement represented a degree of integration of the split-off parts. Even after the patient made this statement, she regressed periodically to the split position over the next months of treatment. The therapist's efforts at that point were to further explore the reasons that these parts of her were split-off.

58. What are some of the early problems that may be encountered in carrying out the treatment? I—Testing the frame/contract

Patients often agree to the treatment contract but are not convinced that therapists will hold to what they have said. Therefore, patients may begin therapy by presenting an intense challenge to the therapist in the form of a challenge to a part of the contract. In terms of the patient's dynamics, this challenge usually represents a conflict between a wish to control or defeat the therapist and an underlying wish that the therapist prove strong enough to withstand the challenge. In "lower level" borderline patients (characterized by extreme narcissism, malignant narcissism, or antisocial personality), the wish to control or defeat the therapist may be stronger than the wish that the therapist exhibit strength. In contrast, in "higher level" patients the wish that the therapist hold fast may be stronger. Nevertheless, in either case, what therapists see is an intense challenge which can test not only their belief in their method but also their ability to tolerate the strong affects elicited in working with borderline patients.

Example: F.E. started therapy after a hospitalization that had been precipitated by an overdose. Her history included numerous other overdoses and frequent cutting. Prior therapies had not led to any noticeable change. When setting up the treatment contract, her therapist, Dr. D., emphasized the need for F.E. to take responsibility for her safety, to call for emergency services if necessary, and to accept to be hospitalized if that was recommended. F.E. initially said that she would never accept admission to a psychiatric hospital again because she found them degrading. Dr. D. explained the reasoning behind his position, but F.E. held to hers. Dr. D. then explained that if they held two different opinions on this important issue, it would not make sense for them to enter into a therapy together. In response to this, F.E. said she would accept the conditions of treatment even if she was not happy with them.

Two weeks after the contract was settled and the therapy had begun, F. E. took an overdose and was brought to an emergency room and admitted to a medical unit of the hospital. The next day, when she was medically cleared, the hospital psychiatrist recommended she be transferred to a psychiatric hospital for further treatment before going back to outpatient treatment. The patient refused this recommendation. The hospital psychiatrist called Dr. D. to inform him of the situation. Dr. D. asked the hospital psychiatrist to remind F. E. of their contract and of the fact that he could not be her therapist if she refused the recommendation for admission to a psychiatric hospital. Hearing this, F. E. had her husband call Dr. D. from her bedside on the medical unit. First the patient's husband and then the patient herself exhorted Dr. D. to take her back into treatment. They accused him of abandoning his patient; they attacked his professionalism; they accused him of being selfish and irresponsible; they threatened him with a lawsuit if any harm came to her. In addition, the patient's husband appealed to Dr. D.'s understanding of what a financial burden their share of a hospital bill would be. Throughout this, Dr. D. reminded the patient and her husband that he was practicing therapy in the best way he knew. He explained that good therapy cannot take place in an atmosphere of risk-taking and that he must respect the opinion of the consulting hospital psychiatrist that a period of time in the hospital was important to sort out what was involved in this overdose.

In spite of his belief in what he was saying, Dr. D. was upset internally by the accusations of abandoning a patient. He knew that if the patient did not return to therapy with him, the hospital psychiatrist would have to arrange an outpatient treatment before discharge from the hospital. However, Dr. D. feared that the likelihood of a good alternative treatment arrangement being set in place in the atmosphere of tension and urgency the patient was creating was small. Although Dr. D. was tempted to deviate from the contract and agree to see the patient, he believed that doing so would render any effective treatment impossible. If he showed at the beginning of the therapy that either he did not believe what he said or that he did not have the conviction to hold to it, the patient would feel, perhaps rightly, that her threats could always overpower his better judgment. In a situation like that, the therapist abandons his role and enters into a relationship where he is reacting to the patient, whose internal dynamics then determine the course the relationship takes.

Dr. D. had to end the phone conversation with F. E. and her husband without having reached a resolution of the situation. He said that all the arguments on each side had been stated and made it clear that he was not changing his position. He left F. E. with the choice of what to do and asked that she call him later in the day to inform him of her decision. Her husband called later to say that she had accepted admission to a psychiatric hospital. When the outpatient therapy resumed, it continued to be characterized by intense and often chaotic affects, but these were within the frame of treatment where they could be contained and explored.

This example shows only one of many ways in which a patient might test the contract. Other possible tests include not attending regularly, not paying, not abstaining from alcohol, and not speaking in sessions. In any one of these situations, the therapist must appreciate the importance of holding to the contract and understanding the meaning of the challenge to it. *Unfortunately, the therapist's holding firm during a first test of the treatment contract does not mean there will not be further tests.* A number of factors play a role in this. One is the patient's natural resistance to the process of internal integration. A second factor is some patients wish to be stronger than the therapist and to triumph over the therapist even at the expense of their own improvement (the malignant narcissism factor). A third is any ambivalence the patient may sense in the therapist. Therapists appearing to waver in their own adherence to the contract may encourage the patient to continue to present challenges to the contract. This is one of the reasons that participation in a supervision group is highly recommended for therapists practicing TFP. The group may help the therapist see the importance of holding to the contract and maintaining the frame at times when the therapist is tempted to "give in."

59. Early problems II—The meaningful communication is subtle and is in the patients' actions more than in his or her words.

A particular problem often arises after the contract is set and the therapy begins. The problem is that the most meaningful communication may be in the interaction of the patient with the therapist rather than in what the patient is saying. The solution to this problem is for therapists to focus on and "read" the interaction and have the confidence to propose a hypothesis based on this reading even if they are not totally sure of its accuracy.

Example: B. C. started therapy upon discharge from the hospital. His hospital admission had been precipitated by a suicide attempt. Diagnostically, he presented with both borderline and narcissistic personality disorders. He was trying to establish himself as an author and had experienced some early success, publishing a story in a respected magazine. This led to his being taken on by a well-known literary agent with whom he became friendly. He attempted suicide after an angry outburst at the literary agent led to that person's ending their contract to work together. B. C. felt he had ruined all his chances for success and was currently consumed with envy for anyone he perceived as achieving any success. B. C. had been brought up by a mother whose social activities had consumed most of her time and a father who was preoccupied with building up his career.

B. C.'s initial attitude toward therapy was skepticism. Now age twenty-four, he had had therapy on and off since he was fourteen. Nothing had ever helped and he agreed to it now because his hospital psychiatrist had strongly recommended this therapist as a specialist. B. C. began therapy saying that suicide was his most attractive option. He would call his parents and frighten them by describing his wish to "blow his brains out." They in turn called his therapist, who arranged a joint meeting with the patient and his parents to make sure everyone had a clear understanding of the diagnosis, the risks, the patient's responsibility for seeking emergency help if needed, and the fact that, although there was no guarantee, there was a good chance for improvement.

As therapy proceeded after this meeting, B. C. became increasingly uncomfortable in sessions and acknowledged that he was developing "a crush" on his therapist. She responded by empathizing with how difficult it appeared to be for him to say this, particularly because he appeared to experience her as completely indifferent to him [identification of the object representation]. For example, B. C. became uneasy in the minutes before the end of each session. His therapist suggested that he experienced the end of the session as proof of her indifference. After a week's interruption in the therapy for the Christmas holiday, B. C.'s participation in sessions became limited to one theme: therapy was "stupid" and "useless" and was only a waste of his time and money. *He would make these statements and then be silent.* The therapist initially responded by addressing the patient's denial of the seriousness of his condition, especially his chronic suicidality. It was as though that had evaporated from the patient's consciousness and therapy itself had become the problem. As the therapist heard herself making these statements, three things occurred to her: 1) she was trying to convince the patient by rationally arguing with him, a strategy which rarely succeeds; 2) there was some truth to the patient's position that the therapy had become the problem—in fact, that is what one expects with TFP: the problem enters the therapy as the patient experiences the transference—and then one has the opportunity to work on it; and 3) the patient's repeatedly falling into silence after declaiming how stupid and worthless therapy was constituted an action which needed to be understood and interpreted. Part of the understanding of his falling silent was based on her countertransference and led to the following intervention:

> I think something is going on here. Your saying that I'm not helping you and then falling silent seems to me to be an implicit request for me to do something—more specifically, an implicit request for me to take care of you. It makes sense

that you would want that when you describe a life where you feel no one has ever taken care of you. It would also make sense that you cannot express that wish/request directly because you feel that it will never happen and that I am completely indifferent to you. It is easier for you to retreat into a cynical rejection of me and of therapy than to acknowledge what you appear to be feeling underneath—a deep wish that I care about you and take care of you. Even though it seems like a long time ago, especially in the climate of this session, we should not forget that a few weeks ago you said you had a crush on me. Your more recent dismissive attitude can be understood as a reaction against that, an attempt to run away from the humiliation you feel because you have begun to care deeply for me and you can't imagine that I would care in any way about you.

The patient nodded in recognition to this intervention. This single intervention did not, of course, resolve the problem, but it opened up the discussion to the core issue—that in the patient's internal world, there was the wish for a care-taking object, but no possibility of finding that object in reality. Because of this assumption, any object experienced as caring became the subject of suspicion. This paranoid stance poisoned the patient's relations with others as it had with his literary agent. An initial good feeling in a relation was inevitably replaced anger when the patient interpreted some action—such as the ending of therapy sessions—as proof that the other did not really care about him.

While this example involves many issues, we use it here to illustrate the therapist's attention to and use of the patient's actions, in this case his becoming silent, as an essential source of information.

60. Early problems III—The therapist has difficulty with how important the therapist has become to the patient.

In the above example, after the therapist centered the discussion on the patient's feelings for her, B. C. began to elaborate on his rationalizations as to why he believed she could not care about him. First, he was convinced she was just seeing him for the money. Second, he was sure that all her patients fell in love with her and he was just like an object on an assembly line to her. As B. C. spoke, his therapist saw more clearly how strong his feelings had become for her over the first three months of treatment. Some therapists are uncomfortable with this reality. In these cases, therapists may deny how strong the patient's feelings are for them and deflect these feelings onto others in the patient's life. In the case of B. C., a therapist with this difficulty might not have picked up on the fact that the patient's attacks on the therapy were defending against a growing attachment. The therapist might have focused on how others have disappointed the patient, missing the point that the intense feelings are in the here and now.

A therapist's discomfort with the strength of the feelings the patient has for him or her may lead to denial and deflection of these feelings. The patient may experience this response of the therapist in two different ways (or in a combination of the two). The patient may collude with the therapist's denial, feeling relieved that the affects are being shunted out of the room. In this case, the therapy may continue for an indefinite period with little getting done. Alternatively, the patient may be horrified that what he most fears has materialized: his feelings are met with a bland denial and a rejection. In this case, the patient is likely to drop out of the therapy.

In order to do the work of TFP, the therapist must accept the fact that the relation with the patient is a real relationship. It is a relationship unlike any other in the patient's life. It is defined with clear limits to the nature of the interaction, but this is not done to limit what the patient feels in relation to the therapist, but rather to allow the patient to experience the full range of his or her most intense feelings in relation to the therapist. Patients often defend against the intensity of their feelings in relation to the therapist by saying

This isn't a real relationship. It's just a professional relationship.

The therapist can point out the defensive nature of this sort of statement by noting that the feelings that develop between two people in any setting are real even if there may not be the possibility of acting on those feelings.

61. How does the therapist manage affect storms?

There are two types of affect storms. The first is the open, direct type in which the patient explodes with expressions of intense aggression, often of a demanding quality. The patients are driven to action, such as yelling or pacing around the room, and their capacity for cognition and reflection is diminished. The second type looks like the opposite on the surface—the patient is withdrawn into a rigid, controlled silence. If the therapist should try to intervene, this silence may be broken by a burst of the more direct affect storm. In either type of affect storm, nonverbal communication and countertransference are the dominant sources of information for the therapist.

The therapist's approach to affect storms should be based on the principle of interpreting the action, although with certain special emphases. First, because of the violence of the affect and the potential for in-session acting out, there must be an emphasis on the frame, with a clear sense of the boundaries of the therapeutic setting in terms of what is tolerated and what is not. Second, it is appropriate to acknowledge the intensity of the affect and to precede any intervention by asking patients if they feel they would be able to tolerate a comment from the therapist at that point. If patients reply that they do not want to hear anything from the therapist, it is appropriate to remain silent (unless any boundaries are being violated) and to interpret later what the reasons might be for the patient's intolerance of any communication from the therapist. The therapist's capacity to tolerate the intensity of the patient's affect without reacting (although countertransference forces can be very strong and must be analyzed) are related to Winnicott's concept of *holding* or Bion's concept of *containing*. The therapist's capacity to integrate, by interpretations, a combined understanding of the patient's behavior and the therapist's own countertransference also contribute to the holding or containing.

The therapist's interpretation should permit the transformation of acting out into a representational experience, a linking of affect and cognition in terms of the clarification of the relationship between self and object that the patient is experiencing and reacting to in the moment. The description of the presently activated object relation also involves the description of the corresponding primitive defense(s), especially projective identification. However, in the midst of an affect storm, the patient may not be able to accept any interpretation, especially of projective identification, and may tend to perceive it as an assault or accusation from the therapist. If this is the case, it is helpful to follow Steiner's recommendation[1] to interpret the nature of what is projected as "analyst-centered," or we might say *object-centered*, spelling out the patient's perception of the therapist in great detail ("You feel I'm the most coldhearted, uncaring bastard in the world."), without either accepting it or rejecting it. This gradually facilitates the patient's tolerance of what the patient is projecting and also clarifies the nature of what is projected and the reasons for it before bringing the interpretation of the projection back to the patient. A typical dynamic of affect storms is the patient's unconscious identification with a sadistic object who only grants its love if the patient self-destructively submits to it. The affect storm may represent the patient's identification with this sadistic object and the projection of the submissive self onto the therapist, even though the content of the patient's remarks may be that the therapist is the bad one.

Therapists should also be aware of the level of affect in their own interventions (this is something therapists should always be aware of, but even more so in the context of an affect storm). While avoiding getting into a shouting match, the therapist should speak with a strong and firm tone that corresponds to some degree to the intensity of the patient's expression of affect. For the therapist to respond with the quiet, bland tone that is a caricature of therapeutic neutrality may only further enrage a patient who is likely to

---

1. J. Steiner, *Psychic Retreats: Pathological Organization of the Personality in Psychotic, Neurotic, and Borderline Patients* (London: Routledge and The Institute of Psychoanalysis, 1993), pp. 131–134.

experience it as a sign of indifference and lack of engagement. In addition, it is extremely important that therapists feel safe in their interventions. To be afraid of patients is a powerful message that only increases the patient's fear, and, sometimes, the rage that defends against their own fear of their potential destructiveness.

An important complication is the danger of affect storms spilling over from the sessions into the patient's life outside of the sessions. In some circumstances, it may be important for the therapist to set limits to the patient's behavior outside the hours or, in extreme situations, to intervene directly in the patient's life. For example, if a patient stormed out of a session saying that she would come back and then did not appear for the next session, the therapist would first call the patient (see Part VIII, question 65 regarding the threat of a patient dropping out). If the therapist were unsuccessful in his attempts to reach the patient, the therapist should call the patient's spouse to alert that person that the patient may have dropped out of treatment and that the spouse may want to do what he or she can to direct the patient back to therapy or to another treatment. Any such departure from neutrality will have to be interpreted and understood later on.

Some patients may learn how to use affect storms as part of an effort of omnipotent control to frighten family members and the therapist, eventually paralyzing the therapist in a fearful avoidance of dealing with particular issues. If therapists are aware that they avoid certain issues with a patient and cannot work this through themself, they should seek supervisory help.

Sometimes a severe transference acting out and an apparently unrelated urgent life situation seem to occur simultaneously, the emotional crisis in the hour emerging in parallel with the emotional crisis in the patient's life outside the session. Patients in this sort of double affect storm create a chaotic situation in which therapists may find it difficult to orient themselves. The therapist should first decide, session by session, what seems most urgent. If the crisis in the patient's life situation indeed has an urgent dangerous quality, it should be explored fully while keeping in mind that the patient may be using the outside crisis to activate or avoid issues in the transference. In some cases, it may be helpful to suggest a temporary increase in the frequency of sessions to have more time to deal both with the emotional crisis in the patient's life and its transference implications. The risk in offering the higher frequency of sessions is the secondary gain involved. If the patient begins to show a pattern of using affect storms to obtain secondary gain, this must be interpreted.

62. What are the signs of progress in TFP?

It should first be said that discussion of progress can create acute anxiety in borderline patients who tend to be rejection-sensitive and can interpret any mention of progress as a sign that the therapist is planning to "get rid of" the patient. Therefore, it is often best for the therapist to note progress internally before making any mention of it to the patient.

The following are indications of progress:

a.) In the first phase of treatment, the patient's acting out decreases in the patient's external life and the atmosphere in sessions becomes more affectively intense,

b.) The patient's comments indicate reflection on and exploration of the therapist's interventions,

c.) The patient can begin to tolerate some awareness of the patient's hatred, and of the patient's love,

d.) The patient can tolerate fantasies that represent the development of an internal psychological space where affects can be consciously experienced rather than discharged immediately into action,

e.) The patient is able to accept the interpretation of primitive defense mechanisms, to take back the projection and to begin to experience the two sides of the split,

f.) The predominant transference evolves from paranoid to depressive, with the associated capacity to experience guilt and gratitude as the patient enters the depressive position.

63. What are signs that the patient is nearing the termination of therapy and how does the therapist conceptualize and discuss termination?

The above indications of progress are all relevant to considering when a patient is ready for termination. The most important indicator of readiness for termination is evidence of intrapsychic integration that is sustained over a period of time. Evidence of this sort often is seen around separations. This is logical since much borderline pathology manifests itself around separations. Issues of separation are related to issues of mourning and it is important to consider the patient's capacity to successfully mourn over the course of the therapy. Part of the initial pathology is the inability to mourn the idealized object. Part of the ongoing pathology is the inability to accept the losses that are inevitable in life because of the way loss is experienced—as total loss of the object with no stable internal representation. Borderline patients often experience separation—even the end of a session—as a rejection and total loss (although very narcissistic patients may defend against this by experiencing and expressing a total indifference on the surface.) The other is not leaving them temporarily, but rejecting and abandoning them. The rage they experience in response to this then attacks the internal representation of the other, risking its destruction, and leaving them feeling empty.

Part of the preparation for eventual termination is to work on the patient's anxieties and fantasies around separations, whether they be provoked by the end of the session or the therapist's vacation. The work around these issues evolves with the desired progression from the paranoid transference and position to the depressive position. In the former, patients experience the therapist as someone who uses or abuses them and then disposes of them, leading to rage around separations. As patients—by virtue of interpretations, their experience with the therapist and perhaps the resolution of narcissistic defenses—begin to be more aware of the therapist's capacity to provide help to them, they generally experience more characteristics of the depressive position. Patients feel that it is the weight of their needs that has exhausted the therapist and kept the therapist from being infinitely available. Patients experience guilt over this "badness" and feel they deserve to be left. Discussion and interpretation of these fantasies help the patient accept the realistic limitations of what the therapist, and others, can offer and help the patient understand that these limitations are due neither to the therapist's meanness nor to the patient's badness. With this awareness, and a realistic mourning of the ideal object, the patient can enjoy the gratifications of real relationships without reacting in catastrophic ways to their frustrations. The patient can experience annoyance and anger over frustrations without totally rejecting and attacking the object. Patients now can experience guilt for aggressive affects without feeling worthless and can experience gratitude without feeling totally beholden to the other. They can maintain stable internal representations of others that are not subject to destruction when they experience a negative affect.

On a practical level, the advanced stages of therapy that precede termination may involve defining and addressing neurotic level issues, such as guilt or ambivalence around sexual feelings or around success. It is up to the therapist to decide to what degree the therapist will work on these issues before terminating with a patient who has resolved the major borderline issue of integrating a split internal world. Another option is to terminate and to allow the patient a period of time (at least six months) to see how the patient experiences and organizes his or her life after having resolved the internal split organization. After that period, the patient could consult with the therapist to determine if it would be helpful to engage in a therapy or psychoanalysis geared to addressing neurotic level issues.

Some of the issues that emerge in the later phases of therapy may have to do with life choices that the patient made when he or she was functioning at a borderline level. Patients often question their choice of partner or spouse. They may have chosen someone they fantasized would be their savior, or their persecutor (a choice more likely based on unconscious motivations), or someone they felt they could exploit as a caretaker. Having entered into a world of more realistic and more mutual relations, their choice may now seem unsatisfactory. In such circumstances, it is important for the therapist to explore to what degree the patient's experience of the spouse may still be based on an unintegrated object representation and also to what degree the devaluing of the spouse may be the counterpart to some continued idealization of the therapist. On some occasions, referral to a specific other form of therapy, such as marital therapy, can be helpful in addressing these issues.

Discussion of termination usually emerges from the therapeutic dialogue as both patient and therapist note the change that has taken place. When the therapist feels it is time to propose termination, the therapist should allow for six more months of therapy before termination to deal with the issues that it brings up. It is important in considering termination to avoid the expectation that all the patient's life problems be resolved. Aiming for perfection could be a way to deny and indefinitely postpone termination. Therapists may join patients in an avoidance of termination since termination brings up issues for therapists as well. Therapists often feel some combination of guilt (experienced as a concern that the patient will not survive without them), loss, and a mix of gratification and sadness (that the patient has "grown up" and can survive without them).

Termination from TFP does not preclude further contact between patient and therapist. The therapist lets the patient know that the therapist is available for future consultation, although, as mentioned above, it is best to have at least a six-month break (except if an emergency arises) so that the end will be real and not a pseudotermination.

Part VII

SOME TYPICAL
TREATMENT TRAJECTORIES

64. Is it possible to delineate some typical treatment trajectories that illustrate TFP principles as the therapy evolves?

One of the complicating factors in treating borderline patients is that the diagnosis covers a broad range of different clinical presentations (see Part I, Diagnostic Issues).[1] Some patients may be more dependent, passive, and depressed. Others may be more fiery, chaotic, and aggressive. Still others may be more detached and schizoid. Nevertheless, clinical experience shows that many patients fall into broad patterns in terms of their treatment trajectories. We will review some of the more typical of these. It should be noted that these trajectories are not mutually exclusive and a patient may exhibit elements of more than one of these.

---

1. J.F. Clarkin, J.W. Hull, & S.W. Hurt, "Factor Structure of Borderline Personality Disorder Criteria," *Journal of Personality Disorders* 7 (1993): 137–143.

A. The patient with a chronic paranoid transference who desperately fights his underlying longing for attachment.

An example of this type is the case of F. E. The first part of her history was described above in Part VI, question 58, "Testing the contract/frame." When the treatment continued after her hospitalization, F. E. approached therapy with the following attitude:

> I'm here because I want to get over my crazy actions and reactions which keep me from being strong. I want to be strong so that I don't have to depend on anyone. You can't depend on anyone. People are just sharks who use and take advantage of each other. My problem is that I'm not good at that. I'm weak and vulnerable. I get upset and hurt myself. I want to get over that so that I can be strong, make a lot of money, leave my husband and live all by myself with as little connection to anyone else as possible.

Dr. D.'s response to this was that it did not seem to tell the whole story. While he believed that she felt as she said, he also believed that there were other feelings in her which conflicted with those. He based his conviction on evidence that she at times appeared to feel close to her husband and at times appeared to feel that way toward Dr. D. himself, as, for example, when she lingered at the end of sessions and appeared not to want to leave. F. E. held to her position, stating flatly that Dr. D. was wrong and did not know her. The two months of therapy after her hospitalization were characterized by this discussion, with other themes also entering into the sessions. Other typical themes were her feeling she was inadequate as a mother and that she was stupid. F. E. linked these themes with her claim that she just needed to be stronger. She continued to act out at times by cutting herself superficially on her arms and legs. She reported that she did this to "relieve tension" but did not appear curious to understand these behaviors any further.

Three months after the beginning of therapy, Dr. D. went away for a week. He had notified F. E. a month in advance. She expressed indifference to his going away and even mocked him for making a big deal of it. When he returned, F. E. reported that her week had been routine, no better or worse than average. Dr. D. was relieved internally. Another two months went by with essentially similar themes to what had preceded. Then Dr. D. announced that he would be away again for a week. This time the patient's reaction was different; she exclaimed: "You can't go away!" as if her saying it would control him. Dr. D. was seeing the breaking through of the split-off side of the patient's internal conflict. Over the months he had worked with her, an intense attachment had developed. F. E. had succeeded in denying it until now. The emergence of this material in such a dramatic way gave Dr. D. more data to support his interpretation that F. E. was torn internally by a terrible conflict between wanting to be attached and cared for and wanting to be independent and dismissive. However, the work on this internal split continued to be intense and challenging.

F. E. acknowledged that she may experience some wish to be close, but pointed to Dr. D.'s going away as confirmation of her stronger wish to extinguish those feelings and become totally independent:

> You see, I'm right. I can't count on anyone. You're going away . . . just when I was beginning to trust you. How can you do that? You're just like everyone else. You wait until I need you and then you disappear. It's like you want to hurt me.

Dr. D. attempted to work on the patient's need for a *perfect* object to feel she could trust any object and included discussion of the role of her aggression in her experience of abandonment:

> **We can now understand better the difficulty you have letting yourself experience the longing for attachment you have. If there is any flaw, any deviation from a perfect attention to you, you experience that as proof that the other person doesn't care at all. At that point, I suspect something more happens; you react with anger and rage at the disappointment**

> you feel and you attack the image of the other person in your
> mind. For instance, it is true that I am going away. But instead
> of holding on to the image of me that you have in your mind,
> your rage wipes out that image, leaving you feeling alone and
> empty. I think, in the end, that it's not my leaving for a week
> that is leaving you feeling totally empty so much as it is your
> attacking the image of me you have in your mind.

The kind of discussion encapsulated in the above remarks by
the patient and therapist can continue for a long period—months
to years—in the therapy. Of course, there are variations and there
is evolution, but the struggle between the patient's internal representations and more realistic and integrated representations of self
and others usually is a slow one.

F. E. continued to accuse Dr. D. of being "just like everyone
else" in disappointing and even betraying her, and yet she continued to come to therapy diligently, suggesting a side that felt
differently. Dr. D., rather than try to convince her he was genuine
and trustworthy, tried to explore her transference in depth: if he
did, indeed, want to gain her trust only to trick and hurt her, what
was his motivation for this? Was he dishonest in presenting himself
as a therapist who wished to help her? Was he perhaps sadistic,
getting pleasure from the suffering he witnessed in her? Sometimes the patient was able to see on her own that some of these
ideas seemed extreme and not to correspond to the reality of
Dr. D.'s being available to her on a consistent basis, as he had
defined in the beginning of the treatment. Yet, at other times, the
reality of the situation seemed to matter little, and F. E. experienced
an occurrence such as the end of a session as proof of Dr. D.'s
indifference to her. This alternation between a distorted perception
and a more realistic one can continue for long periods and requires
the therapist's patience and repeated interventions that address all
the data coming from the three channels of communication.

A.1. How does the therapist integrate material from the past into the focus on the transference?

As therapists draw out the patient's internal representations as they emerge in the transference, they can use material from the past to inform their understanding of representations of others. However, in doing so, therapists are careful to remember that the description of the past they are hearing is what the patient has internalized and not an objective representation of a past reality. This is not to say that the patient's descriptions are not connected to the past reality. However, the unintegrated structure of the borderline patient's psyche may result in characterizations that are partial and contradictory. Therefore, the therapist refers, for example, to "a mother who . . ." rather than saying "your mother." In the case of F. E., the therapist knew that the patient's mother had recurrent depressions and would drink and take drugs rather than seek treatment when she was depressed. In discussing F. E.'s conviction that he was indifferent, Dr. D. would make reference to this part of the patient's internalized past in describing the object representation that was active in the transference at those times:

> **You are reacting to me as though I am a doped up mother who is totally unresponsive to the needy girl in front of me. Your experience of me is of somebody who is inexpressive and expressionless as if he were doped . . . and who only reacts under extreme circumstances. This may be replicating the experience of a thousand interchanges with a doped mother.**

These references to the internalized past enlarge the discussion to allow for elaboration of internal images as they relate to the remembered past and also to elements of the past which may have been suppressed or repressed. Some of the past may emerge as it is relived in the transference without conscious memories of it. It may be through the reliving in the transference that the patient gains awareness of some parts of his internal world and thus becomes more able to integrate those parts into a more meaningful and complete sense of self. However, linking material in the transference with internalized images from the past does not necessarily, in and of itself, lead to integration or resolve conflicts.

For example, F. E. agreed with Dr. D.'s references to "a doped up mother," but this did not immediately resolve her intensely negative transference. She responded:

> *I live twenty-four hours a day replicating those thousand interchanges; I can't get away from it! Only in church if someone's praying for me do I feel relief for a minute.*

Her reference to church provided Dr. D. with more data with which to address her internal split:

> **It is as though you can only believe in someone's care and concern for you in a setting defined as pure goodness, and even then the good feeling is very transient. If there is any ambiguity or uncertainty, as in most life situations—including this one, you switch to your "default" position of experiencing the other as cold and indifferent—"doped."**

One reason that linking the transference to the internalized past does not necessarily lead to integration is, of course, that the internalized images are partial and split from one another. F. E., like many patients, could shift from a negative image of her mother to an idealized one:

> *But she was an invalid . . . what could you expect from her? I knew she wanted the best for me. There must have been something wrong with me that I couldn't make her happy. I'm just too stupid . . . I am now and I was as a child.*

The therapist is again required to adhere to the basic strategy of following the reversals of self- and object-representations and the defensive shifts in dyads.

Eventually F. E. showed evidence of integration of her internal world. In fact, her own words after a year and a half of therapy were like a layman's description of Melanie Klein's concept of moving from the paranoid-schizoid to the depressive position:

> *I know now that people aren't perfect. Maybe it's that I had high standards, but now I've realized you can't find somebody perfect. But I wanted that fairy-tale love that makes you high. I always believed it could happen . . . it has a few times, but it can't stay that way forever. It breaks my heart. I'm the most romantic person . . . if I care, it's 500%.*

This quote communicates a higher level of awareness, and also the sadness that accompanies relinquishing the ideal object.

B. The patient whose aggression is split-off from consciousness and emerges only in action.

Some patients have histories of violent acting out but with no conscious awareness of experiencing aggression. An example is the case of L. S., a young man aged twenty-four at the time he began TFP. His referral came after a serious suicide attempt by overdose. During the ensuing hospitalization, L. S.'s therapist of the past three years suggested that he be referred to a more specialized treatment in place of the supportive psychotherapy they had been engaged in.

L. S. had been in therapy a number of times since his first suicide attempt at age fifteen. Since then he had been hospitalized numerous times after numerous other suicide attempts. L. S. was the only child in a middle-class New England family. His parents were considered eccentrics in the community because of their "hippy style." They were critical of societal norms and encouraged a kind of "freedom" and "equality" in the household that included L. S. calling them "Sally" and "Jim" rather than "Mom" and "Dad" from an early age. The parents also practiced nudism at home and often had L. S. sleep in their bed and bathe with them until his puberty. His father was subject to angry outbursts and sadistic behaviors such as hanging up a bird feeder in the backyard and shooting the birds that came to feed there. Perhaps in contrast to this, L. S. developed a special interest in animals and volunteered at an animal shelter, helping care for abandoned and injured animals. His father relentlessly criticized L. S. for being sissy-like and once shaved the boy's head so he would look like a marine.

L. S. began therapy with Dr. Z., who set up a treatment contract including the patient's responsibility to seek emergency intervention if he could not control his suicidal impulses. Another part of the contract had to do with L. S.'s history of alcohol abuse and the need to remain sober and attend AA meetings. The patient appeared cooperative and expressed his eagerness to "really use" the treatment since he had been told it was more specifically geared to his problems than his prior therapy. The first theme that emerged was L. S.'s difficulty at school. He was attending pre-med courses on a part-time basis and felt paralyzed by anxiety in the classroom. After the first month of therapy, L. S. went to the emergency room and was hospitalized for suicidal ideation. He stabilized quickly in the hospital and was discharged after three days. Dr. Z. tried to explore what feelings were involved in the increased suicidality that led to the hospitalization. L. S. said his hospitalization may have had something to do with adjusting to the new therapy. He had been used to calling his former therapist when distressed and realized that he would now have to deal with this himself. But he said he would get used to Dr. Z.'s ways and that he wanted to "move on with his life and do something about" the anxiety that paralyzed him in his courses. Dr. Z. had the impression that the patient was talking in a superficial way without much affect and pointed this out. L. S. again said that he just needed some time to get used to Dr. Z.

A month later, L. S. went again to the emergency room and was hospitalized for suicidal ideation. It was again a brief hospitalization with quick resolution of the suicidal feelings. Dr. Z. was more concerned than after the first hospitalization. Even though L. S. was adhering to the contract, these hospitalizations suggested that something important was split-off and not getting into the therapy. He soon saw more evidence of this when L. S. began to talk about the new girlfriend he had met in AA. She was a medical student and he believed this would be a positive relationship for him since he too hoped to go to medical school. The next week, however, L. S. revealed that his new girlfriend was helping to pay her way through school by selling drugs to her fellow students. He had decided to join her in this to get out of the debt he was in and help pay for therapy.

Dr. Z. confronted L. S. with the destructiveness of the choice he was describing. He discussed both the risk and also the corruption of the therapy insofar as he planned to pay for therapy with income obtained both illegally and in a way that harmed others.

L. S. replied that Dr. Z. was "out of touch" and did not know what student life was like these days. Dr. Z. felt the issue needed to be understood further but felt it was important to set up a parameter first. He believed the drug dealing was incompatible with therapy and explained to L. S. that he would have to choose between the two. The patient became angry, saying that he had just met this great girl, that she did a little drug dealing, and Dr. Z. had no right to interfere with that. Dr. Z. encouraged him to consider everything he had said and the session ended on that note.

The next day, Dr. Z. received a call from a doctor in the emergency room stating that L. S. had come there and had cut both his wrists badly while waiting to be evaluated there for suicidal ideation. This time the patient's hospital stay was longer and Dr. Z. arranged to have a session with him in the hospital. At the beginning of the session, he told the patient that he wanted to hear about the events that led up to the admission but that it was also important to discuss whether he had decided to accept the new treatment parameter regarding the woman he had met and her drug dealing.

L. S. started with the hospitalization:

What you told me in the last session upset me very much. I think you're a good therapist, but you don't give me much. Ellen [from AA] is the first woman I've met in a long time to really be interested in me. You were forcing me to choose. I kept going back and forth, but couldn't get anywhere except I was getting madder and madder that you were putting me in this position, like I was going to blow up. I went to the ER. . . . They're such idiots there. I was pretty agitated so they put me in the psych room with this guard who had to stay within arm's length of me. I picked up a magazine and pretended to be reading while I slipped out a razor I'd hidden in my wallet. You should have seen it! Moving the magazine just the right way, I managed to cut both wrists until I was bleeding onto the floor with this guy right beside me! You should have seen his face when he first noticed blood! He didn't know if he should run out of the room for help or stay with me so I wouldn't do more.

Dr. Z. felt it was important to comment on L. S.'s affect:

> I'm wondering if you're aware of the feeling you're express-
> ing as you tell me this. It looks like a kind of glee—connected
> to humiliating that guard and showing that he's not doing his
> job. It's important to pause here and think about what's going
> on. There are a number of things, but one of the main ones is
> that you're getting pleasure out of making that man suffer—
> that could be due to a lot of things. It could be a way to get
> back at me for feeling I'm not doing my job, since I'm not
> available the way your prior therapist was. It could be a
> pleasure in turning the tables, since you've so often felt
> humiliated. It could be a simple pleasure in flexing a kind of
> sadistic muscle in you, which is something you have trouble
> acknowledging. Sadistic feelings are pretty common and it's
> not necessarily so bad to have them. The real problem is to
> not be consciously aware of them—then you don't have much
> control over what you do with them. A lot of what's got you
> into trouble, and into hospitals, has to do with this.

After an initial angry reaction, L. S. agreed with what Dr. Z.
was saying. He acknowledged feeling a rage at Dr. Z. in response
to the parameters he set up in the therapy. He agreed that his
defiant plan with Ellen was, at least in part, to show Dr. Z. how he
would "take care of himself" in response to his feeling that Dr. Z.
was not doing so. He further acknowledged that this form of
"taking care of himself" was a two-pronged attack aimed both at
Dr. Z. and at himself. Dr. Z. asked why L. S. would attack himself
if he were angry at his therapist. L. S. could not find a reason
except to say it was "his nature" Dr. Z. proposed they explore this
further but offered two initial hypotheses. The first was that L. S.
might attack himself because of guilt associated with the attack
on Dr. Z. The second, not mutually exclusive of the first, was that
L. S. might attack himself to pre-empt anticipated retaliation from
Dr. Z., in which case L. S. would at least be in control of the
aggression directed toward him.

After this session, L. S. agreed to give up his relationship with Ellen and to continue with Dr. Z. After this hospitalization, the therapy continued without further interruptions due to hospitalizations for uncontrolled suicidal ideation or self-destructive actions. The split-off aggressive feelings that had characterized the first months of treatment were now part of the verbal process of the therapy. L. S. could acknowledge what he had previously put into actions and could also acknowledge an element of pleasure in his aggression.[2]

---

2. Therapists should treat such material non-judgmentally since, from a psychoanalytic point of view, the aggressive drive is universal and can be an acceptable source of pleasure if directed appropriately or sublimated.

C. The patient who controls the therapy.

Some patients have years of therapy and yet demonstrate no change. One reason that this outcome may occur is that some patients experience a strong need to control every interaction, including therapy. In a setting where the "basic rule" is for the patient to free associate, patients can go on indefinitely with a controlling discourse if the therapist is not alert to the importance of the overall interaction as the therapist perceives it in communication channels 2 and 3.

S. P. began therapy with a bang. She walked into the therapist's office for the first consultation session and, before she even sat down, she was talking nonstop about an incident that had just offended her on the subway. The therapist had to talk over her to remind her that this was a consultation session and that he could not address a specific problem with her because he had not discussed the nature of her problem or agreed on an approach to treatment. Dr. U.'s efforts to structure the session and carry out a structural interview were frustrated by the patient's repeatedly ignoring his questions and engaging in a monologue about whatever was bothering her at the moment.

After three such consultation sessions, Dr. U. sought help from his supervision group. The group's recommendation was that he was obtaining the information he needed from the interaction with the patient and that he could proceed to attempt to establish a treatment contract with S. P. without all the explicit data usually obtained in the structural interview. The contract sessions were a challenge but Dr. U. managed to present his understanding that S. P.'s main difficulty was a personality disorder with strong narcissistic features and that the treatment would require their agreement on certain conditions. Aside from the universal aspects of the contract, the principal specific parameter for S. P. had to do with the need for her to engage in a structured, productive activity. During the six months prior to treatment, S. P., who had a college education, had been staying at home and watching television.

Dr. U. proposed that she engage in either studies or some form of work, at least on a part-time basis, as a condition for this type of therapy. S. P. told him that she would never do that and that he could forget about his therapy. Dr. U. recommended that she think about it and that they discuss it further in the next session. S. P. began the next session by announcing that she had obtained a volunteer job on a half-time basis.

The therapy began. S. P. continued as she had begun, flooding Dr. U. with a torrent of discourse. Her main theme was that she was constantly mistreated because of her ethnic background. She provided endless examples of mistreatment and continually made the point that she could never succeed in life because of the animosity others held toward her.

Dr. U.'s thoughts centered on three things:

1. She was flooding him with material—was this an implicit request/demand that he fix her?
2. Yet every time he spoke up, she disregarded him and spoke over him. This suggested that narcissistic issues—the need to be in control and be right—predominated over dependency issues, at least for the moment.
3. His experience was of being mistreated, of being treated rudely and with no consideration, just as S. P. complained she was treated by others.

Trying to follow the treatment strategies, Dr. U. felt he could begin to name the actors. He tried to point out that S. P. was treating him in a devaluing, inconsiderate way. However, the patient gave no indication of reflecting on what he said. Her typical response was to escalate her examples of how people treated her badly and to suggest that Dr. U. was just like everyone else because he was not listening to her.

Because she kept talking over him, Dr. U. decided after a number of sessions that, rather than address the content of what S. P. was saying, he had to focus solely on her style of interacting and the defense it represented:

You know, I find it hard to focus on what you say, and, in fact, I think there is more important information being communicated in how you are saying it—how you are interacting with me. Your non-stop talking seems to be a way to try to control me, and I think it would be important to try to understand why you feel the need to control me. Do you have any thoughts about that?

S. P. angrily replied that she was just doing what he had asked her to do—to say whatever came to mind, and that he was now demonstrating what she always knew, that he wasn't really interested in what she had to say.

Dr. U. commented:

We might have the answer right there. You're convinced that I'm not interested in you, that I don't care. Someone who believed that might want to control the interaction for fear that if she were not in control, she would lose the other.

S. P. replied:

Of course I'd lose your interest. Even my parents weren't interested in me, so why should you be?

Dr. U. pointed out that S. P. was not even allowing herself the chance to find out if he was interested in her. By controlling the interaction to create a "semblance of" interest in her, she maintained indefinitely the belief that he was not. And beyond that, she was remaining unengaged with and thus indifferent to him, since her monopolizing the interaction did not allow him to be in the room as a full-bodied person for her. He existed there like a two-dimensional cardboard cutout that she controlled.

After these comments, there seemed to be a dialogue in the room for the first time. S. P. could acknowledge that she did not allow Dr. U. to "exist" in the room and that this was because of her fear that she could not then control him and he would not be there for her. The dialogue developed the idea that this strategy left her alone, without him in this case, a condition that she had blamed others for.

After this positive session, S. P. returned to treatment with much the same style of interaction that she had presented from the beginning. Dr. U. had to return again and again to the interpretation of her omnipotent control and the fear it represented. It was only after repeating this interpretation many times, in the context of a relationship where S. P. allowed herself to sense Dr. U.'s interest in her, that S. P.'s behavior began to change and her capacity to "let Dr. U. in" and listen to him increased.

When the therapeutic dialogue was thus established, S. P. could then begin to see what Dr. U. had tried to point out at the beginning, that she treated others as she complained they treated her. Her complaints of mistreatment decreased as she was able to see her hostile, controlling role in interactions. Subsequently, she began to report more positive interactions with others at her job. This work took place in the first nine months of her therapy. S. P. required further time in therapy to deal with paranoid concerns that anyone who got to know her intimately would ultimately reject her.

The three cases we have presented thus far as "typical trajectories" offer a sense or flavor of the way patients can present at the beginning of treatment and evolve over the course of treatment. These cases do not provide a complete picture of the different situations and treatments that a therapist might encounter in working with this patient population. The case that follows demonstrates the particular difficulties of a patient with strong antisocial features.

D. The patient with a narcissistic personality and prominent antisocial features who begins therapy with a psychopathic transference.

"Psychopathic transference" refers to a situation in which the patient *acts* in a dishonest and deceptive way toward the therapist and *also projects* those attributes onto the therapist. Addressing a patient's conscious, deliberate deceptiveness is a high priority in treating borderline patients (see Part IV-B, question 41). Many therapists have difficulty empathizing with the psychopathic transference and therefore must be watchful for resistance they may experience in acknowledging to themselves or to their patients that their patients are lying to them or treating them deceptively. A central aspect of the therapeutic approach to psychopathic transferences is to tactfully but directly confront the patient with the deceptiveness.

Unless a patient has a full-fledged antisocial personality disorder (see Part II, question 15), there generally exists an intrapsychic conflict between split-off parts, one representing a desire for honesty and another attacking and corrupting that desire. Narcissistic patients with psychopathic transferences generally reveal a sadistically infiltrated, grandiose self that opposes the weaker but healthier part of the self that desires a dependent relation with an other. Honest communication in the treatment is rendered difficult because of the patient's assumption that any closeness or commitment is deceptive and dangerous. These patients project their aggressive fantasies and wishes onto the therapist. They therefore assume that only deceptiveness protects them from the attacks or exploitation and from the sadistic criticism or devaluation they expect from their therapist. These patients assume that any interest the therapist expresses in them is false and a cover for exploitation and/or attack. Since these patients assume that their therapist must be like them, they experience the initial phase of therapy as a game: Who will outwit whom? Who will be superior to and devalue the other? This stance provides no hope of a genuine relation or a resolution of the conflict within them.

If a case like this advances at all, the patient must begin to realize that the pervasive corruption of human closeness, dependency, and commitment he or she brings to a relationship renders any change impossible. Patients who come to realize this gradually begin to understand that openness is necessary for any change. However, the prospect of openness then exposes the patient to the danger of attack, criticism and rejection. The patient's dilemma is that any openness, any letting down of their defiant contemptuous guard leaves them feeling dangerously exposed to criticism or attack from the therapist. From the therapeutic point of view, this weakening of the patient's guard and increase in their fear and overt suspiciousness is an advance. It represents the evolution of the psychopathic transference into a paranoid transference. The paranoid transference can then be worked through as the therapist explores the internal origins of the patient's suspiciousness of the therapist.

Case Example

This example illustrates how a patient with strong antisocial features may not present with the "typical" self-destructive behaviors considered the "classic" borderline symptoms. Nevertheless, these patients fall clearly within the spectrum of borderline personality organization because their psychological functioning is based on splitting and because they suffer from identity diffusion even while they present to the world a narcissistic grandiose self.

As is typical for patients who come to treatment with problems of antisocial behavior, G. D. was referred by her parents. Mr. D., a prominent attorney, called Dr. T. and appealed for help with his 22 year old daughter. She would have been arrested for repeatedly writing bad checks if Mr. D. had not intervened. In addition, she had lost her most recent job because she had lied to her employer. Mr. D. felt she needed help to "get her on the right path." It was with hesitation that Dr. T. agreed to see the prospective patient in consultation: the antisocial behavior was a bad prognostic sign.

G. D. presented as superficially eager for treatment:

I know I messed up. I just want to move on with my life. All my friends are getting rich, and I'm fucking up." When asked what she felt was "messing up" her life, G. D. replied "bad judgment" and blamed it on her parents because of the chronic bitter discord in their marriage and because of her father's repeated infidelities: "How could I know what to do in life with models like that?"*

The fact that G. D. took no responsibility for her actions concerned Dr. T. He took a thorough history of antisocial behaviors. G. D. reportedly had done well in school until 7th grade when she entered a private school where she considered herself "poor" in comparison to her many affluent classmates. She made a great deal of money in high school by providing drugs to her classmates. G. D. enjoyed fancy restaurants and expensive clothes. Her parents did not keep close enough track of her to question how she afforded her lifestyle. G. D. reported that although she sold drugs, she was too smart to get caught up in regular drug use. Nonetheless, she acknowledged trying the marijuana, cocaine, heroine and ecstasy she sold to her peers in order to see what the experience was like. She denied alcohol abuse. She also denied any history of theft, arrests, violence toward others, torturing animals or setting fires.

G. D. lost touch with her high school friends when she started college. In the new setting, her way of trying to make friends including lying about her background and her family's financial status, and trying to impress classmates by inviting them to expensive restaurants and clubs. It was in paying for these outings with bad checks that she got into trouble with the law. Dr. T. was concerned by the lack of any sign of remorse. Her blame again shifted to her parents. Her statement "They brought me up this way; they should pay so I can live like they do" reflected her parasitic dependency. The patient's behavior also included incurring multiple parking tickets and speeding violations while using her mother's car. With regard to interpersonal relations, she reported having had a number of boyfriends—the longest for a year—but added that she had not been in love with any of them. She described her sexual experiences as "satisfactory" without elaborating. She denied any history of sexually promiscuous behavior.

Dr. T. was concerned about the differential diagnosis of Antisocial Personality Disorder versus Narcissistic Personality Disorder with antisocial features. He attempted to establish if G. D. cared about anyone in her world—if she had a capacity for empathy—or if she viewed others solely as a means to her ends. G. D. expressed what appeared to be a degree of genuine affection and concern for her mother, whom she saw as a basically good person who had suffered because of her husband's domineering and egotistical nature. G. D. felt that her father essentially "got away with murder" the way that he bullied and used others.

With the impression that the patient had some capacity for empathy, Dr. T. made a tentative diagnosis of Narcissistic Personality Disorder with antisocial features. This diagnosis allowed for a guarded prognosis as long as the treatment was carried out with a high level of structure [*N.B., a rule of thumb is that "the lower the level of borderline pathology, the higher the need for structure in the therapy."*] In preparation for a discussion of their respective understandings of her difficulties, Dr. T. asked G. D. how she understood her problems. She repeated that she "didn't have good role models." Dr. T. asked if the patient was interested in hearing his impression and then proceeded to provide a layman's understanding of personality disorder [see Part IV-A, question 26], including mention of narcissistic issues such as a grandiosity and bravado that attempt to cover over a low sense of self. Dr. T. went on to explain that therapy would involve twice-weekly sessions that would call on the patient to join in an effort to grapple with understanding aspects of herself that were difficult to acknowledge and deal with. He added, in anticipation of the treatment contract, that because of the patient's history of lying, the treatment would have to take place in conditions where the therapist be free to communicate with either of the patient's parents, or any other person who might be in a role to verify important information about the patient during the course of the therapy.

Dr. T.'s contract with G. D. included not only that she attend all sessions but that Dr. T. alert her parents any time she did not attend. It also included random drug screens since the therapist felt it would be naïve to take at face value the patient's report that she never used drugs or alcohol. The contract also stipulated that the patient cease any illegal activities, such as writing bad checks, speeding or getting parking tickets. The pro-active parts of the contract were that G. D., who was intelligent, obtain a job and begin to repay her debt to her parents while she went through the admissions process necessary to re-enroll in college. G. D. agreed to the terms of the treatment contract, but sounding hollow and ungenuine in a way typical of a patient with this diagnosis. Dr. T. then scheduled a meeting that included the patient's parents to explain the treatment approach and their role in it. In this meeting, he emphasized that the nature of G. D.'s difficulties put her at high risk of returning to antisocial behaviors. This was in part because she experienced herself as above rules and laws, and in part because she put quick gratification of her desires above any long-term goal. G. D.'s parents were disappointed that Dr. T.'s prognosis was not more optimistic but they appreciated the fact that Dr. T. was involving them actively in the therapy, in contrast to their daughter's prior therapists.

Once begun, G. D.'s therapy had a rocky start. She had a tendency to fill sessions with either trivial information about her daily life or complaints about her parents. There was no indication in her discourse that she had serious problems to work on. In addition, she missed an average of one out of every four sessions in the first two months. Dr. T. felt he had to address the issue of the frame first, reminding the patient of her need to be there and confronting her with the contradiction between her stated interest in treatment and her actions. She replied with hollow-sounding excuses and reassurances about her commitment to treatment. Dr. T. concluded this combination of early non-compliance, the patient's lack of motivation, and the psychopathic transference required reinforcement of the structure from the outside. He called a family meeting to discuss what response might best address the patient's behavior. It was agreed that every time G. D. missed a session without a valid reason, she would lose the use of her mother's car for the next week. Although the patient complained of being treated like a child, she had little choice but to accept the condition. It is only in working with patients with strong antisocial traits that therapists would accept to work in these circumstances where the patient's agreement with the treatment frame is not fully voluntary.

G. D.'s reaction to the family meeting revealed important transferential material. The patient, who had thus far expressed little interest in Dr. T., wondered why he cared whether she attended or not. She knew he was paid for sessions she missed, and wouldn't he like to be paid for doing nothing? Dr. T. asked for her further thoughts on the subject. G. D. supposed that Dr. T. was afraid of her father, that he feared if he charged for too many missed sessions, her father would stop paying for the therapy. This gave Dr. T. the opportunity to understand and elaborate a principal object-relations dyad. On the one hand, G. D. felt that Dr. T. was interested in her only for what he could get out of her, that he was essentially exploitative and that he would "take her for all she was worth." On the other hand, she felt that Dr. T. might be functioning out of fear and intimidation. These were the only two options: he was ruthlessly using her or he was fearful and intimidated. Dr. T. presented this understanding to G. D. and summarized:

> "For you, the world is divided into just two types of people: the strong, who are powerful bastards, and the weak, who act out of fear of the strong."

For the first time, G. D. looked up with an apparent interest and said:

"That's exactly right!"

Dr. T. continued,

"You keep trying to be one of the strong, but you fuck it up."

G. D. again looked understood and had a sense that what Dr. T. was saying might be useful; she suspiciously asked:

"What do you think you'll get out of telling me this?"

The patient appeared surprised that Dr. T. was saying something that seemed relevant and meaningful. Of course, he had struggled to do so before, but the patient's generally empty discourse rendered the task difficult. This was the first time that G. D. acted as though Dr. T. might not be either the mercenary hired by her father or an idiot she could string along indefinitely with empty talk. But if he was not either of those things, she did not know what to make of him, arousing both suspicion and curiosity in her.

This emergence of a paranoid transference was something of a turning point in the treatment and led to moments of authentic dialogue as the patient acknowledged her confusion regarding Dr. T. Nevertheless, the therapy advanced, as most do, with episodes of regression. In the course of G. D.'s therapy, a major setback occurred when the patient was caught shoplifting and was brought to the local precinct and charged. Her parents had to provide bail for her release. The incident appeared in the local newspaper. Dr. T. expressed his concern that the continued antisocial behavior and breach of the treatment contract put the usefulness of the therapy in question. G. D. responded that her arrest had been an experience of "hitting bottom" that "knocked sense" into her and made her realize that it was "now or never": she realized that she was not above the law and that she must either get serious about her life and her treatment or her life would be a failure. Dr. T. was not clear if this was meaningful or empty talk.

In the meanwhile, in the wake of the patient's arrest, her sister did not invite her to her daughter's baptism. This rejection became the chief topic of the next three sessions. The patient virtually lectured Dr. T. about how her sister was "beneath humanity . . . kicking her when she was down . . . betraying family loyalty." This black and white view of the situation—G. D. as the innocent victim of her unethical sister—seemed so preposterous that Dr. T. was aware of a contemptuous element in his countertransference. He related this to the paranoid transference:

> "Your point of view here is so skewed. . . . Maybe your sister *is* acting in a harsh, uncaring way, but your total omission of having any role in this situation is beyond credibility. It's almost as if you're asking me to come out and criticize or reject you for such an unreasonable position. It once again reminds us that you're in familiar territory when a relation is based on suspicion and antagonism. The prospect of working together continues to arouse anxiety in you. What is important here is to look at *why* you care so much that your sister didn't invite you. It may be that you're trying to turn her into the 'bad guy' to take the focus off you. However, there may be more to it than that. Part of you may genuinely care about being accepted, but you feel that's the weak part that makes you vulnerable, so you go on the attack rather than let that part of you show. It's been the same here most of the time: a relationship, as you see it, between enemy camps. In the first part of therapy, your talk seemed to be empty and pointless. I think that was a way to try to control the situation and to control me—like with a stun gun—to keep me from controlling you. But as we've been able to observe and discuss your suspiciousness, it seems that part of it is fear of being rejected. I would propose that you think about how that position may hurt you more than it helps you. That is what is most likely to perpetuate and guarantee rejection, in the name of protection through counterattack and control."

An interpretation like this, even if accurate, will not, in and of itself, convince the patient that she can feel safe in a relationship. However, it may appeal to the patient's observing ego in a way that promotes the patient's considering the possibility of perceiving relations in a different way.

Part VIII

COMMON COMPLICATIONS
OF TREATMENT

65. How does the therapist deal with the threat of the patient dropping out of treatment?

The fact that borderline patients tend to drop out of treatment at a high rate has been well-documented.[1,2] A drop out rate of 20% over a year of treatment is considered favorable.[3,4,5] To understand the drop out problem, and how to address it, it is helpful to understand that various factors may contribute to it. The urge to drop out of treatment can result from:

a.) The negative transference; the patient "deposits" hated internal representations into the therapist and then attempts to separate from them by leaving treatment,

b.) Narcissistic issues;

    i. Patients experience feelings of competitiveness and envy in relation to the therapist, feel humiliated in relation to someone they experience as superior because of the therapist's capacity to help them and thus flee therapy both to get away from these feelings and to "defeat" the therapist,

1. A.E. Skodol, P. Buckley, & E. Charles, "Is There a Characteristic Pattern to the Treatment History of Clinic Outpatients with Borderline Personality?" *Journal of Nervous and Mental Diseases* 171 (1983): 405–410.

2. F.E. Yeomans, J. Gutfreund, M.A. Selzer, et al., "Factors Related to Drop-outs by Borderline Patients: Treatment Contract and Therapeutic Alliance," *Journal of Psychotherapy Practice and Research* 3 (1994): 16–24.

3. M.M. Linehan, H.E. Armstrong, A. Suarez, D. Allmon, & H. Heard, "Cognitive-Behavioral Treatment of Chronically Parasuicidal Borderline Patients," *Archives of General Psychiatry* 48 (1991): 1060–1064.

4. A.E. Bateman, P. Fonagy, "The Effectiveness of Partial Hospitalization in the Treatment of Borderline Personality Disorder: A Randomized Controlled Trial," *American Journal of Psychiatry* 156 (1999): 1563–1569.

5. J.F. Clarkin, P.A. Foelsch, K.N. Levy, J.W. Hull, J.C. Delaney, & O.F. Kernberg, The Development of a Psychodynamic Treatment for Patients with Borderline Personality Disorder: A Preliminary Study of Behavioral Change, (*Journal of Personality Disorders*, in press).

      ii. The patient experiences jealousy with regard to the therapist's other patients and other interests,

c.) Dependency issues; the patient becomes anxious because of dependency feelings that development in the positive side of the transference (which may be hidden from view) and leaves therapy to avoid the anxiety associated with dependency,

d.) Fear of hurting the therapist/a wish to protect the therapist; patients feel that their intense affects (aggressive and/or affectionate) are too much for the therapist, or anyone, to bear and decide to leave before this becomes apparent; a milder form of this is guilt or shame over sadistic or libidinal feelings,

e.) Pressure from the patient's family to quit treatment in cases where a change in the patient is perceived as threatening the equilibrium of the family system.

It is essential to address any indication of potential drop out as soon as it appears. Any of the above situations can be addressed with interpretation. In clinical practice, the most common reason for patients to threaten to drop out of treatment is difficulties with dependency and attachment. Patients with a classic paranoid transference—the fear that anyone they get attached to will abandon them, exploit them or otherwise hurt them—have great difficulty as the positive side of the transference grows. They feel very vulnerable in this situation and are prone to see rejection in almost anything the therapist says or does. If therapists announce that they will be away for a week, patients may respond that it is because the therapist is tired of them and they have decided to end the treatment because they know the therapist will eventually leave them anyway. If the therapist looks at the clock, the patient may interpret that action the same way. Patients do not always report these reactions, so if they announce that they are leaving treatment, it is helpful to keep this dynamic in mind and to interpret to patients that the urge to leave treatment may correspond to an increasing attachment that seems frightening and hopeless.

Since the risk of drop out is very high, therapists should actively intervene around it, even if it requires a temporary departure from technical neutrality. For example, if a patient misses a session with no advance notification, the therapist should not wait until the next session to see if the patient comes, but should rather call the patient to inquire about missing the session. The patient's response may range from a bland "I forgot" to announcing that the patient has decided to end therapy. In the former case, the therapist can wait until the next session to explore the forgetting. In the latter, the therapist should not hesitate to make a strong recommendation that the patient come to the next session to discuss what has led to this decision:

> I believe it would be a mistake to break off the treatment now. It is precisely when feelings are running the highest that we stand to make the most progress in understanding them.

If the patient holds fast, the therapist should make the best case for coming:

> While the decision is totally up to you, I strongly recommend that you come in so we can discuss this. You have been in many treatments before and your life is still very difficult, with little reason to believe that things will change without treatment. This therapy is specifically designed to address your problems, but to get any benefit from it, you have to stick with it even when the going gets tough.

If the patient still does not agree to come, he usually says something that gives an idea of the reason that he is leaving treatment; it is usually along the lines of

> *Why should I come anyway? For you, it's just a job, while for me it's a gut-wrenching experience.*

At this point, even though it is not in the context of a session, the therapist may have to follow the rule of making an interpretation if that is the only option left in a crisis situation:

> I think what you just said is important. You can't imagine that I care about you. . . . For me "it's just a job." This situation may be recreating in your mind the situation you have experienced repeatedly and that leaves you feeling so unhappy and hopeless in your life. Somebody begins to be important to you, and you can't imagine that you mean anything to that person, and it's a very painful feeling. I'm not sure about this, but if there's anything to what I'm saying, I think it's a reason to come in and look at this rather than to have the same pattern repeat itself again and again in your life.

In this example, the very fact of the therapist's calling may influence the way the patient experiences him. Since patients typically alternate between a positive and negative transference, it often happens that in the time between sessions the negative transference gets the upper hand. The patient may begin to ask himself

> Why should I trust that guy? He's just like everyone else. I'm just a paycheck for him.

Direct contact with the therapist, who generally communicates an interest in the patient, may challenge this negative view. It is for that reason that a decision to drop out that comes up between sessions should be addressed immediately by the therapist. This contact may connect with or activate the positive side of the transference in a way that will allow the patient to question negative convictions enough to continue the therapeutic dialogue. This example does not cover all the possible issues that may be involved in a patient's decision to drop out, but it illustrates what is probably the most common one.

66. Are patients with childhood sexual and/or physical abuse capable of engaging in TFP?

Yes. To further clarify this question, it is important to keep in mind that studies have shown that not all borderline patients have a history of abuse, and that many patients with other psychiatric disorders and many people without a psychiatric illness in adult life do have a history of childhood sexual or physical abuse. The overall rate of childhood sexual abuse in patients with BPD in a number of studies was about 70%.[6] Most of these studies did not carefully consider the severity of the abuse. Paris' own study[7] looked at the question of severity and found that 30% of the abused BPD subjects in his study had experienced the more severe form of childhood sexual abuse with penetration.

Many stressors and life events, including childhood sexual and physical abuse and neglect, have contributing roles in the development and crystallization of the personality organization. While events themselves may have an impact on the structure of the personality because of a predominance of negative over positive experiences (see Part I, question 8), it is also true that the personality structure, to the extent that it is developed at the time of the trauma(s), determines the manner in which the individual experiences and does or does not integrate the events.

Individuals with a history of abuse who do experience psychopathology in adult life may manifest any of a number of specific psychiatric conditions, including major depression, generalized anxiety disorder, panic disorder, or alcohol or substance dependence.[8] There are also those who suffer from either post-traumatic

---

6. J. Paris, *Borderline Personality Disorder: A Multidimensional Approach* (Washington, DC: American Psychiatric Press, 1994).

7. J. Paris, H. Zweig-Frank, & H. Guzder, "Psychological Risk Factors for Borderline Personality Disorder in Female Patients," *Comprehensive Psychiatry* 34 (1994): 410–413.

8. K.S. Kendler, et al., "Childhood Sexual Abuse and Adult Psychiatric and Substance Use Disorders in Women," *Archives of General Psychiatry* 57 (2000): 853–959.

stress disorder (PTSD) or borderline personality disorder or both. We distinguish these groups although some authors argue that all these patients have PTSD, and that BPD is a misunderstanding of PTSD.[9] We believe, however, that the two groups are distinct. If the diagnosis is PTSD without BPD, the patient should be directed to a treatment specific to that disorder.[10]

If the patient has developed a personality disorder, the pathology can be treated with TFP. In such cases, the therapy is usually characterized by the unconscious activation of the victim-perpetrator dyad in the transference. Patients generally cannot get beyond this dyad as a principal organizer of their on-going life experience because of difficulty in consciously accepting that the internalized dyad includes the perpetrator role along with the victim role. As long as the dyad continues as an *unconscious* psychic structure, it exerts an influence on patients' perceptions and behaviors that is beyond their control. The goal, of course, is to help patients gain awareness of the split-off identification with the perpetrator and the associated aggression so that that part of the psyche can be integrated and thereby lose its extreme and uncontrolled power.

In such cases, patients may accuse the therapist of terrible sadism (if only because of holding to the treatment frame) while expressing (through devaluing remarks or accusations) or enacting (through destructive or self-destructive behavior) aggression that is not consciously experienced as such. It is important in these cases to be especially attentive to the nonverbal channels of communication that express the unacknowledged identification with the persecutor. It is also important to empathize with the difficulty the patient has accepting an identification with a hated figure (although exploration may reveal strong ambivalence toward the figure). However, the patient cannot get better until both parts of the victim-persecutor dyad are "out in the open."

9. J.L. Herman, *Trauma and Recovery* (New York: Basic Books, 1992).

10. J. Chu, *Rebuilding Shattered Lives: The Responsible Treatment of Complex Post-Traumatic and Dissociative Disorders* (New York: John Wiley and Sons, 1998).

Therapists studying TFP sometimes raise the concern that certain characteristics of the therapy might themselves traumatize the patient. They refer to therapeutic neutrality (see Part V, question 54), to the relative lack of immediate gratification, and to the perceived lack of validation. The TFP point of view is, first, that the therapist is very attentive to the *totality* of the patient's subjective state. This means that the therapist both accepts the patient's description of her experience and may suggest that there is more to be aware of. For example,

> I understand that you feel I'm taking away what you need to survive by going away next week, but have you noticed the way you are shaking your fist at me? It may be that the rage that that represents is what is keeping you from maintaining an internal image of me that could reassure you while I am away. It may be that your rage, which you do not seem to be fully aware of, is keeping you from having a sense of connection to me more than my going away is.

While pointing this part of the patient out to her may be distressing to the patient in the moment, it can lead to an integration and resolution of the internal split and its impact on successful functioning. An approach that offered only sympathy with the patient's experience as victim would not empathize with the totality of her internal experience and would reinforce the internal split with its harmful tendency to project aggression onto (an) external object(s) and thus to remain in a paranoid position.

67. Is hospitalization ever indicated in the course of treatment?

It can be. In the current climate of brief psychiatric hospitalizations, this level of treatment is reserved for acute crises when the patient is not able to control intense self-destructive or suicidal impulses. This situation could arise when a patient is experiencing a comorbid major depressive episode, in which case the goal of hospitalization would be to provide the appropriate somatic treatment (medication or, in extreme cases, electroconvulsive therapy) for the depressive episode (see question 69). Alternatively, the need for hospitalization may arise when patients are testing the therapist to see if the therapist will deviate from the contract and become more involved with the patient if the patient communicates difficulty or inability in controlling his or her impulses. In these cases, if the therapist adheres to the contract and recommends hospitalization rather than get more involved with the patient, the need for hospitalization generally decreases or ends all together when the patient realizes that distress calls will not lead to the desired increased contact with the therapist. Very often, patients in TFP stop having hospitalizations (Part X, question 79). This may be due to the fact that hospitalizations interrupt the regular contact with the therapist that most patients in treatment begin to value.

In some circumstances, stressors in the patient's life (e.g., being presented with divorce papers, learning of the suicide of a friend) heighten the patient's distress and anxiety to such a degree that the patient is temporarily less able to control self-destructive or suicidal impulses. In these cases, a hospitalization can provide a safe setting in which to address the immediate stressor and its impact.

The main functions of hospitalization are the following (each of which may be more or less indicated according to the circumstances of the individual case):

1. Reassess the patient's diagnosis or diagnoses,
2. Assess or reassess the need for medication and the medication regimen,
3. Reassess the treatment contract in terms of the patient's
   compliance with it and the possible need to add new
   parameters. Sometimes patients are hospitalized because
   they have not adhered to the responsibilities they agreed to
   in the contract; in these cases, therapists must assess with
   patients if they are willing to make a true commitment to
   the conditions of treatment or if it is better to acknowledge
   that they either cannot or will not do this and that it would
   be better to refer the patient to another form of treatment
   rather than resume TFP after discharge from the hospital,
4. Assess the situation for problems that may have existed in
   the treatment and analyze if these problems can be addressed by either revising the treatment contract or understanding an impasse that may have developed in the
   therapy. Impasses can develop in the therapy when therapist and patient collude in denying or otherwise not
   addressing an affectively charged issue (e.g., an intense
   positive transference or an erotic transference). In such
   cases, the therapist is advised to seek consultation and
   supervision. Depending on the type of problem that exists,
   the therapist might decide to continue with the patient after
   having gained some insight into the problem, to refer the
   patient to another TFP therapist, or to refer the patient to
   another form of treatment.
5. Assess for the possible need for adjunctive treatments such
   as marital therapy or substance abuse treatment (which
   generally requires a hiatus from TFP until the patient has
   achieved a period of sobriety).

Before the advent of managed care, many patients had access
to the option of long-term hospital treatments in settings specialized for the treatment of borderline personality disorder. Such
treatments continue to exist only on an extremely limited basis in

the United States and are not an option for most patients. This form of treatment was very helpful for borderline patients organized at a low level who depend on their primitive defense mechanisms to maintain a degree of stability in their lives, even if this stability is punctuated with periods of decompensation and affect storms. It is a particular challenge to treat these patients in an outpatient setting because as the treatment progresses, the analysis of primitive defenses that is necessary to bring about integration weakens the effectiveness of these defenses. Therefore, a "good" session in which, for example, patients experience some awareness of the intense aggression in their internal world could stir up a level of anxiety and distress in patients that make it hard to transition back to external reality at the end of the session. It is helpful that the therapist communicate empathy for the difficulty of this task.

In some cases, it may be that the patient would benefit from a preparatory treatment before engaging in TFP. Such therapy could be in the form of medication, a course of cognitive-behavioral therapy, skills training, group therapy, family therapy, vocational counseling, or treatment of severe eating disorders or substance abuse.[11]

---

11. H. W. Koenigsberg, O. F. Kernberg, M. H. Stone, A. H. Appelbaum, F. Y. Yeomans, & D. Diamond, *Borderline Patients: Extending the Limits of Treatability* (New York: Basic Books, 2000), pp. 247–266.

68. If the patient is hospitalized, should the therapist meet with the patient in the hospital?

In general it is a good idea for the therapist to meet with the patient in the hospital as long as this does not provide the patient with secondary gain (e.g., if the therapist stopped by the hospital every day to see the patient). Having a session or sessions in the hospital provides an opportunity to consider the issues reviewed in question 67 regarding the reasons behind the hospitalization: diagnostic issues, need for medication, need to revise the contract, consideration of a treatment impasse, need for an adjunctive treatment, or indication for referral to another therapist or treatment. However, if the patient is hospitalized very briefly (e.g., over a weekend) because of concerns about safety and then quickly "reconstitutes," the therapist can explore this in the next outpatient session.

69. What is the role of medications in TFP?

Medications have been shown to help with some of the specific symptoms that borderline patients experience, but they do not treat the personality disorder itself.[12] In addition, studies have yet to provide a clear treatment of choice for a given symptom. The current state of the art in medicating borderline patients is to target symptom clusters with a systematic approach as summarized in the following three algorithms (based on Soloff's work with modifications by Dr. Judit Gordon-Lendvay):

When medicating borderline patients, it is important to keep in mind that the effects of drug treatment in this population tend to be weak and nonspecific, and, after an initial period of effectiveness, often diminish over time. With regard to the treatment of depression, patients with borderline personality disorder who experience a major depressive episode respond less well both to antidepressant medication and to ECT than depressed patients without the comorbid personality disorder.

When treating borderline patients, it is important to distinguish between characterological depression, which tends not to respond to medication, and a major depressive episode. The former has to do with the patient's chronic disposition, based on an internal world including persecutory elements and a subjective experience that does not offer relief from these persecutory, critical, devaluing components. In the context of this subjective experience, it would be unusual not to experience sadness and depression. In contrast, a major depressive episode is marked by very specific neurovegetative symptoms (characteristic patterns of insomnia or hypersomnia, lack of appetite or excessive eating, psychomotor retardation or agitation, poor concentration, lack of sex drive,

---

12. P.H. Soloff, "Pharmacological Treatment of Personality Dimensions: Symptom Specific Treatment for Cognitive, Perceptual, Affective, and Impulsive Behavioral Dysregulation," *Bulletin of the Menninger Clinic 62* (1998): 195–214.

Algorithm 1
Axis II PD with suspiciousness, paranoid ideation, hallucination, mild thought disorder, dissociation*

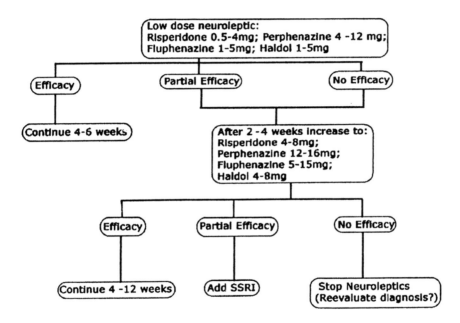

*If major symptom is dissociation then start with SSRI

Algorithm 2

Axis II PD with depressed/angry/anxious/labile mood

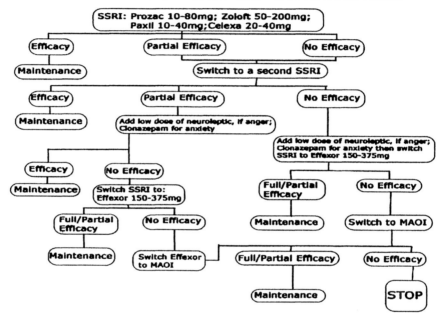

Algorithm 3

Axis II PD with impulsive aggression, self-injurious behavior, binges

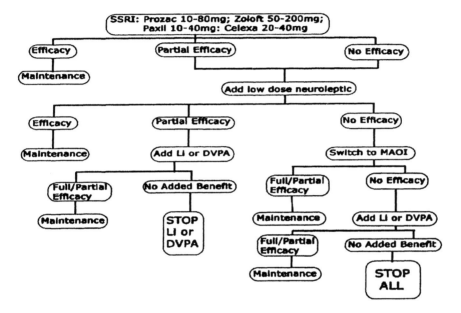

general anhedonia) and unremitting pessimism and hopelessness with recurrent thoughts of death and/or suicidal ideation. While pessimism, hopelessness, and thoughts of death and suicide may be part of a chronic borderline condition and can be addressed with the methods of TFP, the presence of the complete picture of a major depressive episode in a borderline patient warrants a temporary shift in the focus of treatment. This shift involves the appropriate use of medication (prescribed by the therapist or through consultation with a psychopharmacologist—see question 70 below), hospitalization if indicated, and modifications in the treatment contract. The latter are called for in the context of a major depressive episode because the impact of the depressive episode may impair the patient's capacity to take responsibility as called for in the treatment contract. In this circumstance, the therapist may have to be more directive than usual in arranging a psycho-pharmacological consultation, engaging family members to monitor the patient's compliance with medication, instructing family with regard to indications for hospitalization, and/or arranging hospital admission.

Even in light of the above discussion, the management of medication in the treatment of borderline patients remains a subtle and challenging task. The clinician confronts many situations where the characterological versus biological nature of symptoms may remain unclear. In such cases, a trial of medication may be indicated to see if it alleviates the symptom to some degree. Nevertheless, even some improvement in symptoms does not guarantee that the symptom is biological in origin or that it is without psychological meaning. One reason for this is that the placebo effect is a real phenomenon; this may be why borderline patients, who can be very suggestible, often show an initial response to treatment that diminishes over time. Another reason is that what we consider biological and psychological are not entirely separate domains, with more research required to help us understand the interconnections between the two.

70. Who should prescribe the medications?

Non-M.D. therapists have no choice but to refer the patient to a psychiatrist colleague for medication consultation and prescribing. In such cases, it is essential that the therapist choose a psychiatrist who is well-versed in borderline dynamics and, if possible, in TFP. The risk in not doing so is that the situation could become an enactment of the patient's internal dynamics. Most typically this gets played out as the psychiatrist representing the good provider and the therapist, who is generally more careful with limit setting, experienced as the depriving bad object. However, other scenarios are also possible. Sometimes the psychiatrist is devalued as incompetent and experienced as an extension of the indifferent therapist who does not care enough to provide the best treatment. Alternatively, the patient may feel the therapist is referring the patient for medication consultation because the therapist has lost interest in the patient and the therapy. In any case, the psychiatrist should be familiar enough with borderline dynamics to be able to factor the patient's psychological issues into his assessment of the patient's medical condition and to be aware of the potential for the acting out of internal dynamics in the treatment setting. It is especially important that the psychiatrist understand the role of the treatment contract and limit setting in the patient's therapy. A worst-case scenario is a psychiatrist who joins with the patient in devaluing the therapist as uncaring and withholding when the therapist is simply maintaining the appropriate treatment frame.

M.D. therapists have the option of prescribing medication themselves or referring the patient to a colleague for this part of the treatment. A pure TFP model would separate the roles so that the therapist is not obliged to take time during the therapy sessions to do the work of monitoring medication trials or to possibly provide channels for secondary gain if the patient perceives that, for example, reporting side effects of medication is a means to obtain more phone contact with the therapist between sessions. If therapists choose this *split treatment*, they should, as discussed above, be vigilant for the possible enactment of the patient's internal dynamics in the expanded treatment setting.

If therapists choose to do the medication assessment and prescribing themselves, they must be very alert to the many meanings that the prescribing of medication can take on within the transference.

71. What are the most typical transference meanings of medication?

Insofar as any prescribing of medication involves the therapist, or psychopharmacologist, offering something to the patient, the situation is fraught with the potential for transference meanings. These include the patient experiencing the medication as a "magic pill" that is a symbol of the desired omnipotent other. In this case, the patient may report a quick improvement (quicker than possible if it were a true medication effect) followed by an eventual disillusionment when the medication did not provide the wished-for total well-being and then a shift to a negative transference.

Another common response is the patient experiencing any medication offered as "bad milk." In this case, the patient responds to each medication trial with an immediate and intolerable side effect. While it is true that many medications do have side effects, most patients are able to tolerate some degree of discomfort in exchange for the potential benefit of the medication. Patients who immediately reject each medication are likely to be those for whom anything less than ideal care is rejected as inadequate and uncaring (these patients tend to have strong narcissistic features).

Another frequent response to medication is to experience it as the therapist's attempt to offer a "cheap" substitute for true love and caring. In this case, the patient may say:

> You just don't want to be bothered by me. You're just giving me this medication to shut me up and send me on my way.

72. How does one handle crises around interruptions in the treatment?

Many borderline patients have difficulty with any interruption in the treatment (although highly narcissistic patients may present a total indifference to whether the therapist is there or not). Any separation, even the end of a session, can provoke fear of the complete loss of the object. The separation is experienced by the patient as a rejection, the rejection he dreads but expects as inevitable. This rejection provokes a reaction of rage, which may be conscious or unconscious. The rage attacks the internal represen-tation of the abandoning object, destroying it and leaving the patient with a varying combination of emptiness and fear of retaliation and revenge. Because of this cycle, the announcement that the therapist will be away in the future often precipitates a crisis. The crisis may typically take the form of an affect storm and/or of threats to leave the treatment. The reader is referred to Part VI, question 61 to review management of the former, and to Part VIII, question 65 for a discussion of the latter.

73. How does the therapist deal with intense eroticized transferences?

There are more than one type of eroticized transferences.[13] We will focus on two types commonly found in the therapy of borderline patients. The first, more primitive type is challenging because it appears to bring together the libidinal and aggressive sides of the split, yet without any integration. In the normal, integrated psyche, there is a capacity for ambivalence and an integration of libido and aggression. Borderline individuals sometimes manifest a regressive form of pseudointegration in which the aggressive segment of the psyche latches on to aspects of the libidinal segment and recruits them for destructive ends.[14] Love and sexual excitement can be used in the service of aggression in a syndrome of perversity. In therapy, this can take the form of the patient becoming overtly seductive to the therapist, proposing sexual relations or perhaps even to leave their respective spouses to be together. While, on the surface, this may appear to be an extreme manifestation of positive transference, the therapist must be clearly focused on the destructiveness and the attack on the therapy. These situations usually have more to do with issues of power than of love. In some cases, patients may be attempting to use the only attribute they ever felt was valued—their sexual attractiveness— to gain control over a situation that is increasingly distressing. This heightened distress often comes from a sense of being in unfamiliar territory. If the therapist does not play out the expected role of exploiter/abuser, patients have difficulty comprehending the therapist's interest in them. Attempts at overt seduction both return the situation to familiar territory and also place the patient in

13. H.W. Koenigsberg, O.F. Kernberg, M.H. Stone, A.H. Appelbaum, F.Y. Yeomans, & D. Diamond, *Borderline Patients: Extending the Limits of Treatability* (New York: Basic Books, 2000), pp. 193–204.

14. S. Akhtar, *Quest for Answers: A Primer of Understanding and Treating Severe Personality Disorders* (Northvale, NJ: Jason Aronson, 1995).

the exploiter role. The situation is an intense and potentially chaotic one, because as the therapist sets limits and attempts to interpret patients' actions, patients generally experience themselves in the victim role, protesting that the therapist's refusal of their offer is a rejection and proof of their worthlessness.

The second type of erotic transference we will discuss involves patients who have made progress in therapy and who respond to a still partially-idealized view of the therapist with desires which include an erotic component. These patients generally have lived with extremely low self-esteem and one of the principle issues in this type of eroticized transference is the patient's insistence on her unworthiness. The challenge for the therapist is to feel comfortable experiencing in the countertransference whatever feelings of attraction the therapist has for the patient without becoming anxious that allowing such feelings is itself a breaking of boundaries.

These moments can be some of the most challenging in therapy. The patient's expression of interest in the therapist may be direct ("I don't know how to say this, but I've got a crush on you."), joking and ironic ("I know you'd never be seen in public with someone like me."), or indirect and nonverbal. In any case, the most important thing is that the therapist not shy away from the material. Therapists have trouble discussing issues of attraction when their feelings are not of the same intensity as the patient's. However, the most rejecting behavior is to give the message that these feelings are taboo. The therapist should proceed with clarification—can patients say more about their attraction? What are their fantasies? If patients say they cannot proceed, it is too humiliating, the therapist should inquire about their assumptions—why are they convinced the therapist does not like them? What keeps them from imagining that if they met in different circumstances they might not enjoy each other's company? Exploration of these issues usually sheds important light both on the patient's search for the ideal other and on their devaluing of themselves, both of which frustrate their ability to find an appropriate partner in life.

Part IX

REQUIREMENTS FOR DOING TFP

74. What are the basic skills needed to do this treatment?

One of the difficulties in articulating the skills needed to practice
TFP is that each individual patient responds somewhat uniquely to
the process. Thus, the therapist enters the situation of a session
with a general paradigm, but must apply that to the individual
situation. In this context, the basic skills are the following:

a) The ability to be comfortable with the primary process
material that can be part of the activation of internal representations. This is an extremely important capacity for the TFP therapist
and one that is not related to cognitive capacities but to psychological sensitivity. We must remember what distinguishes secondary process from primary process. Primary process is a primitive
form of logic that does not correspond to ordinary logic; it does not
respect ordinary dimensions of space and time. It is a primitive
affect-driven type of logic that does not include the principle of
contradiction. In primary process thinking, highly charged affective relationships and representations of self and other can be
condensed or displaced.[1] Secondary process involves ordinary
ways of reasoning that respect rational logic. The TFP therapist
must be able to tolerate the loss of ordinary logic and its replace-
ment by the activation of intense affect-driven object relations
dyads—some of them fueled by intense desire, others by intense
fear. The TFP therapist must be comfortable with both the primary
process material that comes from the patient and that which is
catalyzed in his own psyche. This material involves affects of
intense fear, rage and hatred, as well as intense longing, love, and
desire. It involves fantasies that range from the most violent to the
most gratifying.

Ideally, therapists can function simultaneously in two roles,
one in which they regress and are immersed in the primary process
material that emerges, and one in which they remain rational and
can observe and comment on this process. Therapists who have

---

1. S. Freud, *The Interpretation of Dreams*, Standard Edition, 4 & 5
(London: Hogarthy Press, 1957).

difficulty with this generally err in one of three ways: 1) therapists are rigidly logical and cannot empathetically regress (these therapists tend to be obsessive), 2) therapists have the capacity to regress but do not have the capacity to resonate empathetically with the deeper aspects of another human being (these tend to be narcissistic), and 3) therapists are so prone to empathetically regress that they cannot keep an observing distance—they are so overwhelmed by feeling that they lose the capacity to reason objectively (these tend to be histrionic).

b) The ability to build a collaborative relationship with the patient.

TFP uses the psychodynamic techniques of clarification, confrontation, and interpretation in the here-and-now interaction, but does not make use of explicitly supportive therapy techniques such as giving advice and praise. That does not mean, however, that the TFP therapist does not make interventions that are experienced as supportive by the patient. Without using explicitly supportive techniques, the TFP therapist builds a collaborative relationship with the patient in a number of ways.

The contract setting early in TFP is a collaborative effort to make clear the roles and responsibilities of both patient and therapist. This definition of roles and responsibilities provides the patient with a framework that is potentially comforting and invites collaboration and cooperation with the therapist.

During the treatment, the therapist never characterizes the patient as totally destructive or totally out of control. Rather, the therapist might refer to "parts" of the patient that are at war with each other.

> **There is the destructive part of you that wants to destroy this treatment by coming to session intoxicated, and there is the healthier part of you that wants to work in treatment and get better.**

Avoiding "all or none" statements about the patient that would reflect how borderline patients talk about themselves and others, and instead referring to different parts of the patient allows the therapist to imply a collaborative effort with the healthier part of the patient.

TFP is also collaborative in the way that interpretations are often made not as definitive truths, but as hypotheses to be considered by both patient and therapist. An interpretation made by the therapist as a hypothesis is a way of inviting the patient's collaborative discussion of the hypothesis and further elaboration of it.

c) The ability to describe the interaction manifested in the treatment room and the patient's attitude that is implicit in the verbal and nonverbal behavior.

d) The ability to observe the contradictions (verbal-verbal; verbal-nonverbal) in the patient's self presentation.

e) The ability to observe and label the patient's dominant affect in the here-and-now.

f) The ability to observe the patient's projection of self and other representations and to accept the projection non-defensively. This includes the ability to experience, in the session, the changing experience the patient is having of you, the therapist, which may be very different from the way you see yourself in the session.

g) The ability to tolerate the possibility that a patient could commit suicide. Once again, not all therapists are comfortable with this possibility. However, if a therapist cannot accept this possibility but agrees to work with a suicidal patient, it is very likely that the patient will control that the therapist and that the therapy will not be able to address important areas that the patient is defended against.

h) The ability to sort out what part of your reactions to the patient comes from your own internal world versus what part of your reactions is provoked by the patient. (see Part IV-B, question 40 on countertransference.)

i) The ability to verbally describe the patient's self-other relationship with the therapist in the here-and-now interaction.

j) The ability to pursue a line of clarification and confrontation, leading to interpretation of the dominant transference theme in a field where more than one theme may be present simultaneously.

k) The ability to pursue a line of interpretation over a period of time even if the interpretation is met with resistance and the progress is marked by periodic regressions.

l) The ability to deepen the interpretation to further levels of the patient's experience to explore what the surface levels of the patient's awareness are defending against at deeper levels of his/her psyche.

75. What forms and levels of supervision are necessary/ advisable?

The TFP therapist must at least have access to consultation and supervision from an experienced colleague or teacher. The ideal situation is to participate in a supervision group that meets on a regular basis. This could be a peer supervision group or a group with a designated leader if one individual clearly has more expertise and experience than the others in the group. It is very difficult to treat borderline patients without the need for periodic consultation. This stems in large part from the nature of projection, projective identification, and countertransference—the nonverbal exchange of primitive material that the therapist is not always able to be conscious of, or sometimes admit to, without help.

Part X

PRACTICAL QUESTIONS
IN DELIVERING THE TREATMENT

76. How does one get consultation on the TFP treatment of BPO patients or organize a supervision group?

The need for consultation or supervision comes up in most cases at some point. Even in those cases where it is not essential in order to resolve a treatment impasse, it can provide reassurance to the therapist that his understanding of the case and his approach to it are on target. It is helpful to know what other therapists in your area have a special interest in treating borderline patients and, if possible, to form a peer supervision group. At the present time, there are TFP centers in New York City; White Plains, New York; Quebec City; Mexico City; Munich; Amsterdam; Leiden, Holland; Maastricht, Holland; and Lausanne, Switzerland. Access to these centers is possible through our website at Borderlinedisorders. com. In addition, we have information about groups that are being formed elsewhere and individuals who are interested in participating in a group in different areas so we may be able to help interested therapists make contact.

77. How does one cover these patients when the therapist is away?

The issue of coverage is related to the question concerning crises around interruptions in treatment (Part VIII, question 72). Since TFP is focused on the centrality of the transference, it would be naive to think that the same sort of work could be done with a "stand-in" as is being done with the regular therapist. Nevertheless, there is a role for coverage. First, it is essential that there always be a covering therapist available in case any crisis or emergency should arise. Beyond this, it is usually recommended that during the first year of treatment, patients be given the clear option of meeting with the covering therapist. These sessions could be just once-a-week. The purpose of these sessions is to continue to provide a structure of treatment during a period when the patient is still working on internalizing that structure and to explore with the patient the experience of his therapist being absent. If life crises arise, they can also be addressed in these sessions.

It often occurs in coverage situations that patients begin to idealize the covering therapist and to devalue their own therapist. One reason for this is that covering therapists are often perceived as less strict with boundaries. Another reason may be that the idealizing transference of the covering therapist may be a way to punish the principal therapist for having gone away.

78. What if I work in a clinic that does not support twice-a-week therapy?

Many therapists work in settings where twice-a-week therapy is considered a luxury. Nevertheless, these clinics often provide a standard once-a-week frequency of therapy for patients even if the patients are being seen for chronic supportive care without the goal of active change. It is our recommendation therapists in these settings assess and triage patients in terms of frequency of visits. The patients who are being seen in a chronic maintenance mode may require less frequent sessions. This could free up time in the therapist's case load to offer twice-a-week therapy to patients who have the potential to effect major change in the setting of a more intensive therapy.

79. Is there empirical data to show that TFP is effective?

Our clinical research group has studied intensively the treatment of a group of female patients with BPD. The symptoms, functioning, and service utilization of these patients for the year prior to their treatment with TFP was compared to their behavior in these realms during the year and at the end of one year of treatment in TFP. Patients were assessed at baseline and at the end of twelve months of treatment with diagnostic instruments, measures of suicidality, self-injurious behavior, symptomatology, social functioning and interpersonal relations, and measures of medical and psychiatric service utilization.

Retention-attrition. For those completing the treatment contract, the one-year attrition rate was 19.1% (4 of 21 of patients dropped out of treatment) and no patient committed suicide. This drop-out rate compares well with Linehan's study[1] (4 of 24, 16.7%, one suicide, 4%), Stevenson and Meares' study[2] (16%), and Bateman and Fonagy's study[3] (21%). There was a tendency for the treatment decliners to live farther from the institute, although this difference did not reach statistical significance. None of the treatment completers deteriorated or were adversely affected by the treatment. Therefore, it appears that TFP is quite well-tolerated.

Suicidal and self-injurious behavior. There was a significant reduction in the number of patients who had made a suicide attempt in the year prior to treatment (53%) compared to the number who made an attempt during the one year of treatment

---

1. M.M. Linehan, H.E. Armstrong, A. Suarez, D. Allmon, & H. Heard, "Cognitive-Behavioral Treatment of Chronically Parasuicidal Borderline Patients," *Archives of General Psychiatry 48* (1991): 1060–1064.

2. J.E. Stevenson, R. Meares, "An Outcome Study of Psychotherapy for Patients with Borderline Personality Disorder," *American Journal of Psychiatry 149* (1992): 358–362.

3. A.E. Bateman, P. Fonagy, "The Effectiveness of Partial Hospitalization in the Treatment of Borderline Personality Disorder: A Randomized Controlled Trial," *American Journal of Psychiatry 156* (1999): 1563–1569.

(18%). In addition, there was a trend for reduction in the medical risk of these acts. There was a significant reduction in the medical risk and physical condition following self-injurious behavior. Suicidal ideation did not decrease, but there was a significant increase in reasons for living.

One possible interpretation of the combination of these data elements, which is congruent with clinical thinking, is that during the first year of treatment there is an increasing containment of action while suicidal ideation remains. In this context, there is a growing awareness of satisfactions in life and reasons to live. In contrast to the decline in outright suicidal behavior, self-injurious behavior did not decrease in frequency. However, the medical risk of these behaviors was significantly reduced, and the physical condition of the patients were improved.

Symptoms. Self-report measures of suicidal ideation, depression, anxiety, and anger were utilized in this study along with a global assessment of multiple symptom areas. The measure of global symptoms significantly decreased as did state anxiety. There was a trend for depression and trait anxiety to decrease. Anger, both in state and trait form, did not change.

Social adjustment. As a group, these patients made significant positive changes in friendships and work. In a treatment of one-year duration, these patients did not make significant changes in intimate relations. This supports the expectation that a psychodynamic object relations treatment such as TFP would show its influence in the relations with significant others in the environment. It also seems plausible that changes in intimate relations may take longer than one year of treatment.

Cost effectiveness. Although this study was not specifically designed to examine cost-effectiveness nor do we have data on the exact cost savings between the year prior and the treatment year, the dramatic reduction in service utilization in terms of emergency room visits (55% reduction), hospitalizations (67% reduction), and number of days in the hospital (89% reduction; 39.2 versus 4.5 days) suggests a substantial cost savings associated with our treatment.

The results of our findings, as well as those of others[4, 5, 6] suggest that a longer duration of treatment appears to not only be necessary for symptoms embedded in personality structure but also seems to be highly cost-effective with borderline patients.[7]

Study limitations. As a preliminary study, there are a number of design issues that limit the interpretation and the generalizability of our results. First, the absence of a comparison group limits the interpretation of positive change, as the change we observed in our patients may have occurred over time without TFP or even without treatment. However, previous research with borderline patients has found fair stability over two to five year periods in terms of the diagnosis and level of emotional difficulties.[8, 9] Nevertheless, a randomized controlled trial of TFP would constitute a more stringent test of the efficacy of this treatment, and with the positive results presented here we are proceeding to such a study.

The sample in the present study was a relatively homogeneous group of severely disturbed, chronically self-destructive borderline women. It is unclear if our results would generalize to

4. M.M. Linehan, H.E. Armstrong, A. Suarez, D. Allmon, & H. Heard, "Cognitive-Behavioral Treatment of Chronically Parasuicidal Borderline Patients," *Archives of General Psychiatry* 48 (1991): 1060–1064.

5. J.E. Stevenson, R. Meares, "An Outcome Study of Psychotherapy for Patients with Borderline Personality Disorder," *American Journal of Psychiatry* 149 (1992): 358–362.

6. A.E. Bateman, P. Fonagy, "The Effectiveness of Partial Hospitalization in the Treatment of Borderline Personality Disorder: A Randomized Controlled Trial," *American Journal of Psychiatry* 156 (1999): 1563–1569.

7. G.O. Gabbard, S.G. Lazar, J. Hornberger, & D. Spiegel, "The Economic Impact of Psychotherapy: A Review," *American Journal of Psychiatry* 154 (1997): 147–155.

8. L.A. Hoke, P.W. Lavori, & J.C. Perry, "Mood and Global Functioning in Borderline Personality Disorder," *Journal of Psychiatric Research* 26 (1992): 1–16.

9. P. Vaglum, S. Friis, S. Karterud, et al., "Stability of the Severe Personality Disorder Diagnosis: A 2- to 5-year Prospective Study," *Journal of Personality Disorders* 7 (1993): 348–353.

less severely disturbed borderline individuals or whether the treatment would be as effective for men. With regard to the issue of effectiveness with less severely disturbed patients, findings from follow-up studies and uncontrolled outcome studies suggest expressive (psychodynamic) psychotherapy *in general* appears more effective for less severely disturbed borderline patients and that psychological-mindedness, low impulsivity, and good social support appear to predict better outcome from expressive therapy.[10]

Although patients who complete a research protocol may represent a more functional subsample of borderline patients than those who are not able to comply with a study, the patients in this study did represent a group of individuals with severe BPD who frequently harmed themselves, attempted suicide, and were hospitalized, while exhibiting severe levels of depression, and suffering from high levels of symptomatic distress. We cannot yet be sure of the effectiveness of TFP with less experienced therapists. On the one hand, TFP is a relatively sophisticated set of strategies, tactics, and techniques. On the other hand, four of the eleven therapists in our study were trainees and one other was a first year faculty member. However, all therapists in our study, including trainees, had at least one year of experience working with borderline patients and experience working psychodynamically with patients.

Conclusions. This study using the patients as their own controls is highly suggestive that TFP is well-tolerated and may result in considerable improvement in functioning in a broad range of areas. Based on the present findings, future research with TFP is warranted. Future studies should include a randomized controlled trial of TFP as well as exploring the treatment process and underlying mechanisms of action that result in change for these patients. Additionally, given the severity and chronicity of BPD, follow-up data is imperative to establish the long-term significance of these findings.

---

10. A.E. Roth, P. Fonagy, *What Works for Whom? A Critical Review of Psychotherapy Research* (New York: Guilford Press, 1996), pp. 207–209.

A FINAL NOTE

This book has attempted to present a systematic approach to the challenging task of treating borderline patients. We feel that this approach can be of help to the therapist, but ultimately even more so to our patients, many of whom achieve significant and lasting change. However, before ending, it is important to note that a system is the tool of those who use it, and the final decision about what to do in a specific situation with a specific patient remains that of the individual clinician. This book does not present the sum-total of what therapists might find helpful and appropriate to do in working with borderline patients. It should not be otherwise. In our own work, we are aware that we treat individuals, not diagnoses. We have benefited a great deal from using the method presented in the book, but we have also used it as a flexible guideline, to combine with our overall clinical judgment. We offer it as such to our readers.

REFERENCES

PART I

American Psychiatric Association (1994). *Diagnostic and statistical manual of mental disorders (4th ed.)*. Washington, DC: Author.

Bion, W.R. (1961). *Experiences in groups and other papers*. New York: Basic Books.

Clarkin, J.F., Hull, J.W., & Hurt, S.W. (1993). Factor structure of borderline personality disorder criteria. *Journal of Personality Disorders, 7*, 137–143.

Dicks, H.V. (1967). *Marital tensions*. New York:Karnac Books.

Jacobson, E. (1954). The self and the object world. *The Psychoanalytic Study of the Child, 9*, 75–127.

Kernberg, O.F. (1975). *Borderline conditions and pathological narcissism*. New York:Jason Aronson.

Kernberg, O.F. (1976). *Object relations theory and clinical Psychoanalysis*. New York:Jason Aronson.

Kernberg, O.F. (1980). *Internal world and external reality: Object relations theory applied*. New York:Jason Aronson.

Kernberg, O.F. (1981). Structural interviewing. *Psychiatric Clinics of North America, 4*, 169–195.

Kernberg, O.F. (1984). *Severe personality disorders*. New Haven: Yale University Press.

Kernberg, O.F. (1992). *Aggression in personality disorders and perversions*. New Haven:Yale University Press.

Kernberg, O.F. (1995). Omnipotence in the transference and in the countertransference. *The Scandinavian Psychoanalytic Review, 18*, 2–21.

Kernberg, O.F. (in press). Freud conserved and revised: an interview with David Scharff. In: *The psychoanalytic century*. Edited by David Scharff. Old Tappen, NJ: Other Press.

Klein, M. (1957). *Envy and gratitude.* New York:Basic Books.

Skodol, A.E., Gunderson, J.G., Livesley, W.J., Pfohl, B.K., Siever, L.J., & Widiger, T.A. (2000). The Borderline Diagnosis from the Perspectives of Psychopathology, Comorbidity, Personality Structure, Biology, Genetics, and Course. Manuscript submitted for publication.

Weissman, M.M. (1993). The epidemiology of personality disorders. In R. Michels, A.M. Cooper, S.B. Guze, L.L. Judd, A.J. Solnit, A.J. Stundard, & M.M. Weissman (Eds.), *Psychiatry* (Vol. 1, Chapter 15.2, pp. 1–11). Philadelphia: Raven-Lippincott.

PART II

Bateman, A.E., Fonagy, P. (1999). The effectiveness of partial hospitalization in the treatment of borderline personality disorder: A randomized controlled trial. *American Journal of Psychiatry, 156,* 1563–1569.

Bateman, A.E., Fonagy, P. (2001). Treatment of borderline personality disorder with psychoanalytically oriented partial hospitalization: An 18-month follow-up. *American Journal of Psychiatry, 158,* 36–42.

Clarkin, J.F., Yeomans, F.E., & Kernberg, O.F. (1999). *Psychotherapy for borderline personality.* New York:John Wiley and Sons.

Cleckley, H. (1976). *The mask of sanity* (4th ed.). St. Louis: Mosby.

Gabbard, G.O., Coyne, L., & Allen, J.G. (2000). Evaluation of intensive inpatient treatment of patients with severe personality disorders. *Psychiatric Services, 51,* 893–898.

Gunderson, J.G. (2001). *Borderline personality disorder: A clinical guide.* Washington, DC: American Psychiatric Publishing.

Hull, J.W., Clarkin, J.F., & Yeomans, F.Y. (1993). Borderline personality disorder and impulsive sexual behavior. *Hospital and Community Psychiatry, 44,* 1000–1002.

Linehan, M.M. (1993). *Cognitive-behavioral treatment for borderline personality disorder.* New York:Guilford Press.

Monroe-Blum, H.E., Marziali, E. (1995). A controlled study of short-term group treatment of borderline personality disorder. *Journal of Personality Disorders, 9*, 190–198.

Perry, J.C., Banon, E., & Ianni, F. (1999). Effectiveness of psychotherapy for personality disorders. *American Journal of Psychiatry, 156*, 1312–1321.

Rockland, L. (1992). *Supportive therapy for borderline patients: A psychodynamic approach.* New York:Guilford Press.

Stone, M. (1990). *The fate of borderline patients.* New York: Guilford Press.

Waldinger, R.J. (1987). Intensive psychodynamic therapy with borderline patients: An overview. *American Journal of Psychiatry, 144*, 267–274.

PART III

Kernberg, O.F. (1980). *Internal world and external reality: Object relations theory applied.* New York: Jason Aronson.

PART IV-A

Kernberg, O.F. (2001). The suicidal risk in severe personality disorders: Differential diagnosis and treatment. *Journal of Personality Disorders, 15*, 195–208.

Swartz, M., Blazer, D., George, L., & Winfield, I. (1990). Estimating the prevalence of borderline personality disorder in the community. *Journal of Personality Disorders, 4*, 257.

Yeomans, F.E., Selzer, M.A., & Clarkin, J.F. (1992). *Treating the borderline patient: A contract-based approach.* New York:Basic Books.

PART IV-B

Green, A. (1993). *On private madness.* Madison, CT: International Universities Press.

Racker, H. (1957). The meaning and uses of countertransference. *Psychoanalytic Quarterly, 26,* 303–357.

PART IV-C

Steiner, J. (1993). *Psychic retreats: Pathological organization of the personality in psychotic, neurotic, and borderline patients.* London: Routledge and The Institute of Psychoanalysis.

PART VI

Steiner, J. (1993). Ibid.

PART VII

Clarkin, J.F., Hull, J.W., & Hurt, S.W. (1993). Factor structure of borderline personality disorder criteria. *Journal of Personality Disorders, 7,* 137–143.

PART VIII

Akhtar, S. (1995). *Quest for answers: A primer of understanding and treating severe personality disorders.* Northvale, NJ: Jason Aronson.

Bateman, A.E., Fonagy, P. (1999). The effectiveness of partial hospitalization in the treatment of borderline personality disorder: A randomized controlled trial. *American Journal of Psychiatry, 156,* 1563–1569.

Chu, J. (1998). *Rebuilding shattered lives: The responsible treatment of complex post-traumatic and dissociative disorders.* New York:John Wiley and Sons.

Clarkin, J.F., Foelsch, P.A., Levy, K.N., Hull, J.W., Delaney, J.C., & Kernberg, O.F. (2001). The development of a psychodynamic treatment for patients with borderline personality disorder: A preliminary study of behavioral change. *Journal of Personality Disorders, 15*, 487–495.

Herman, J.L. (1992). *Trauma and recovery*. New York:Basic Books.

Kendler, K.S., et al. (2000). Childhood sexual abuse and adult psychiatric and substance use disorders in women. *Archives of General Psychiatry, 57*, 853–959.

Koenigsberg, H.W., Kernberg, O.F., Stone, M.H., Appelbaum, A.H., Yeomans, F.Y., & Diamond, D. (2000). *Borderline patients: Extending the limits of treatability*. New York:Basic Books.

Linehan, M.M., Armstrong, H.E., Suarez, A., Allmon, D., & Heard, H. (1991). Cognitive-behavioral treatment of chronically para-suicidal borderline patients. *Archives of General Psychiatry, 48*, 1060–1064.

Paris, J. (1994). *Borderline personality disorder: A multidimensional approach*. Washington, DC: American Psychiatric Press.

Paris, J., Zweig-Frank, H., & Guzder, H. (1994). Psychological risk factors for borderline personality disorder in female patients. *Comprehensive Psychiatry, 34*, 410–413.

Skodol, A.E., Buckley, P., & Charles, E. (1983). Is there a character-istic pattern to the treatment history of clinic outpatients with borderline personality? *Journal of Nervous and Mental Diseases, 171*, 405–410.

Soloff, P.H. (1998). Pharmacological treatment of personality dimensions: Symptom specific treatment for cognitive, perceptual, affective, and impulsive behavioral dysregulation. *Bulletin of the Menninger Clinic, 62*, 195–214.

Yeomans, F.E., Gutfreund, J., Selzer, M.A., et al. (1994). Factors related to drop-outs by borderline patients: Treatment contract and therapeutic alliance. *Journal of Psychotherapy Practice and Research, 3*, 16–24.

PART IX

Freud, S. (1957). The Interpretation of dreams. *Standard Edition*, 4 & 5. London:Hogarth Press.

PART X

Bateman, A.E., Fonagy, P. (1999). The effectiveness of partial hospitalization in the treatment of borderline personality disorder: A randomized controlled trial. *American Journal of Psychiatry, 156*, 1563–1569.

Gabbard, G.O., Coyne, L., & Allen, J.G. (2000). Evaluation of intensive inpatient treatment of patients with severe personality disorders. *Psychiatric Services, 51*, 893–898.

Henderson, D.K. (1939). *Psychopathic states*. London:Chapman and Hall.

Hoke, L.A., Lavori, P.W., & Perry, J.C. (1992). Mood and global functioning in borderline personality disorder. *Journal of Psychiatric Research, 26*, 1–16.

Linehan, M.M., Armstrong, H.E., Suarez, A., Allmon, D., & Heard, H. (1991). Cognitive-behavioral treatment of chronically parasuicidal borderline patients. *Archives of General Psychiatry, 48*, 1060–1064.

Roth, A.E., Fonagy, P. (1996). *What works for whom? A critical review of psychotherapy research*. New York: Guilford Press.

Stevenson, J.E., Meares, R. (1992). An outcome study of psychotherapy for patients with borderline personality disorder. *American Journal of Psychiatry, 149*, 358–362.

Vaglum, P., Friis, S., Karterud, S., et al. (1993). Stability of the severe personality disorder diagnosis: A 2- to 5-year prospective study. *Journal of Personality Disorders, 7*, 348–353.

RECOMMENDED READINGS

Part I: Who Are The Patients?

Akhtar, S. (1995). *Quest for answers: A Primer of understanding and treating severe personality disorders.* Northvale, NJ: Jason Aronson.

This concise volume provides a comprehensive commentary on the range of personality disorders, covering both diagnostic and treatment issues.

Barron, J.W., Ed. (1998). *Making diagnosis meaningful: Enhancing evaluation and treatment of psychological disorders* (Washington: American Psychological Association).

There is a growing sense among clinicians that the DSM diagnostic system falls short as a guide to treatment for the individual patient. The authors in this volume provide thoughtful alternatives to patient assessment and diagnosis for treatment planning. These attempts are often related to this book's approach to personality pathology that goes into more depth than the DSM's Axis II.

Kernberg, O.F. (1975). *Borderline conditions and pathological narcissism.* New York: Jason Aronson.

Kernberg's first book on borderline personality established the foundation from which TFP developed. It provides an understanding of borderline personality organization that remains as relevant today as when it was first published. The chapters on the treatment of narcissistic personality provide detailed guidance to the clinician working with that challenging subset of patients with borderline organization. This book is being reprinted in conjunction with *A Primer on transference-focused psychotherapy of borderline patients.*

Kernberg, O.F. (1984). *Severe personality disorders: Psychotherapeutic strategies*. New Haven: Yale University Press.

This volume of Kernberg's writings contains essential chapters on the structural diagnosis of personality disorder and the structural interview, a highly organized clinical method of making the diagnosis. Kernberg examines these issues in various age groups such as adolescence and old age, and discusses problems in the classification of personality disorders. Other chapters relate to the treatment of the personality disorders, with one chapter (13) providing a very good clinical example of the therapy of narcissistic personality.

Kernberg, O.F. (1996). "A Psychoanalytic theory of personality disorders," In: J.F. Clarkin, & M. F. Lenzenweger (Eds.), *Major theories of personality disorder*. New York: Guilford Press.

This is a concise and clear description of the basic building blocks of personality and personality pathology from a psychodynamic and object relations point of view. The edited volume as a whole contains chapters with theories written from other points of view by leading personality disorder theorists, e.g., Aaron Beck, Lorna Benjamin, Theodore Millon.

Klein, M. (1957). *Envy and gratitude*. New York: Basic Books.

An essential work in the development of object relations theory with vivid descriptions of Klein's concepts of the paranoid-schizoid and depressive positions.

Jacobson, E. (1954). The Self and the object world. *The Psychoanalytic Study of the Child*, 9, 75–125.

A key work in the early development and elaboration of object relations theory.

Lenzenweger, M.F., Clarkin, J.F., Kernberg, O.F., Foelsch, P.A. (in press). The Inventory of Personality Organization: Psychometric properties, factorial composition and criterion relations with affect, aggressive dyscontrol, psychosis-proneness, and self domains in a nonclinical sample. *Psychological Assessment*.

This is an article on the basic properties of a self-report instrument developed at the Personality Disorders Institute of the Weill Cornell Medical College to measure personality organization in terms of neurotic personality organization and borderline personality organization. It yields scores on constructs of identity/identity diffusion, use of primitive defenses, and reality testing. The instrument may be of use to busy clinicians who want some screening on their patients in reference to personality organization.

Livesely, J., Ed. (2001). *Handbook of personality disorders: Theory, research and treatment*. New York: Guilford, 2001.

In contrast to the approach in this primer, this handbook edited by a leading researcher in the personality field stays close to a DSM-IV, Axis II description of the personality disorders. It is an excellent summary of data on the etiology, development, diagnosis, assessment and treatment of those with personality disorders.

Stone, M. (1990). *The Fate of borderline patients*. New York: Guilford Press.

A necessary step in understanding the nature and mechanisms of a particular type of patient pathology is to examine it across time. Michael Stone followed approximately 500 psychiatric patients who were treated at the New York State Psychiatric Institute for a follow-up period of 25 years. His work provides the best data we have on the long-term course of individuals with borderline personality disorder, grouped according to their most common co-morbid conditions.

Part II: What is the Essence of the Treatment?

TFP

Clarkin, J.F., Yeomans, F.E., & Kernberg, O.F. (1999). *Psychotherapy for borderline personality*. New York: J. Wiley and Sons.

This is the treatment manual that describes TFP from the beginning to end. The book was written over a span of 15 years during which senior therapists were treating borderline patients with our method, videotaping sessions, and discussing them in weekly supervisions. From these meetings, we derived the principles of treatment and collected clinical vignettes that illustrate the principles.

Gill, M.G. (1982). *Analysis of transference, volume I: Theory and technique*. Madison, CT: International Universities Press.

Gill provides a thorough review of the development of the concept of transference in psychoanalysis and its use as an analytic tool.

Other Treatments for Personality Disorders

The interested reader can examine TFP by also knowing about the contrasting treatments, thereby knowing what TFP is and is not. The most articulated treatments for borderline patients other than TFP are the following:

Benjamin, L.S. (1993). *Interpersonal diagnosis and treatment of personality disorders*. New York: Guilford Press.

Keenly aware of the problems with the DSM approach to personality disorders, Benjamin brings the reader back to the interpersonal genesis and context of all symptoms of personality disorder. This orientation is used to guide a sophisticated approach to treatment that has many similarities to the psychodynamic approach.

Gunderson, J.G. (2001). *Borderline personality disorder: A Clinical guide.* Washington: American Psychiatric Publishing.

This review of borderline personality and the various approaches to treating it includes sections on case management, hospital treatment, residential treatment and partial hospital care, pharmacotherapy, cognitive-behavioral therapies, family therapies, group therapy and individual therapies.

Linehan, M.M. (1993). *Cognitive-behavioral treatment of borderline personality disorder.* New York: Guilford Press.

This is a detailed and sophisticated description of borderline personality disorder from a cognitive-behavioral perspective, accompanied by an explication of a one-year treatment. The treatment is defined in terms of strategies and change procedures.

Rockland, L.H. (1992). *Supportive therapy for borderline patients: A psychodynamic approach.* New York: Guilford.

This is a clearly conceptualized approach to the borderline patient that uses techniques of encouraging a positive alliance, furnishing hope and reassurance, providing advice, suggestion and education, making interventions with the patient and family or others in the patient's life, use of medication, and providing a model for the patient's adaptation to everyday life.

Waldinger, R.J. (1987). Intensive psychodynamic therapy with borderline patients: An Overview. *American Journal of Psychiatry,* 144, 267–274.

This article reviewed the major psychodynamic approaches to treating borderline patients and found that, whatever the differences in emphasis or technique, all of these approaches included the following elements: the need for a stable frame of treatment, an increased level of therapist participation in the treatment as compared to therapy with neurotic patients, tolerance of the patient's hostility, attempting to make self-destructive behaviors ego-dystonic, using interpretation to connect actions and feelings, setting limits, focusing early therapeutic work and interpretations on the here-and-now, and monitoring countertransference.

Manualized Psychodynamic Treatments not specifically for Personality Disorders

There have been several previous efforts at describing psychodynamic treatments in a manual form. These treatments are principally targeted for outpatients with general depression and anxiety, and, in terms of our classification scheme, would be for those patients with neurotic personality organization. They are of interest to the psychodynamic therapist in that they describe psychodynamic methods in a more general and less specifically targeted way than we do in describing TFP.

Luborsky, L. (1984). *Principles of psychoanalytic psychotherapy: A manual for supportive-expressive treatment*. New York: Basic Books.

This a book by one of the leading researchers of psychodynamic therapy and one who heralded the coming of the treatment manual as a necessary tool of therapy research. This book describes a psychodynamic treatment for symptomatic outpatients that combines supportive and dynamic techniques. The focus of intervention is on the relationship themes as enunciated by the patients.

Strupp, H.H., & Binder, J.L. (1984). *Psychotherapy in a new key: A guide to time-limited dynamic psychotherapy*. New York: Basic Books.

Time-limited, psychodynamic, and focused on outpatients with symptoms of depression and anxiety, this is another attempt to "manualize" a treatment that focuses on the repetitive themes in the approach of the patient to self and others.

Part III: Treatment Strategies

Clarkin, J.F., Yeomans, F.E., & Kernberg, O.F. (1999). *Psychotherapy for borderline personality.* New York: J. Wiley and Sons.

This is the treatment manual that describes TFP from the beginning to end. The current *Primer* is a distillation and further refinement of the ideas presented in this book. The 1999 volume offers the reader expanded descriptions of some of the key concepts of TFP and provides lengthier clinical examples.

Part IV: Tactics

Yeomans, F. E., Selzer, M.A., & Clarkin, J.F. (1992). *Treating the borderline patient: A contract-based approach.* New York: Basic Books.

One of the most difficult therapeutic tasks in working with borderline patients is at the beginning of the therapeutic relationship. The empirical data are clear in pointing out that borderline patients are more prone than patients with other diagnoses to prematurely end treatment. This book describes a psychodynamic approach to beginning the treatment with borderline patients. This treatment contract or agreement between patient and therapist involves the clear, careful articulation by the therapist of the roles and responsibilities of both parties to the treatment, with discussion between the two of the implications. It is, in the best of circumstances, the beginning of a treatment process that will continue in the face of intense and conflicted feelings with the goal of psychological integration.

Part V: Treatment Techniques

Racker, H. (1957). The meaning and uses of countertransference. *Psychoanalytic Quarterly*, 26: 303–357.

Racker's seminal article offers a detailed discussion of the concept of countertransference and develops the concepts of concordant and complementary countertransference. It also offers rich clinical examples that illustrate the complexity of the interaction between patient and therapist and the need for the therapist to be very attentive as he or she attempts to understand the projections at play in the interaction.

Part VI-IX: Treatment Issues

Diamond, D., Clarkin, J.F., Stovall-McClough, K.C., Levy, K.N., Foelsch, P., Levine, H., and Yeomans, F.E. (in press). Patient-therapist attachment: Impact on therapeutic process and outcome. In: M. Corina & M. Marrone (Eds.), *Attachment and the Psychoanalytic Process*.

The conceptual and empirical work on attachment style is growing. This chapter describes work by our research group with regard to attachment. The work investigates both the impact of attachment style of borderline patients who are in treatment with TFP and changes in their attachment style during the first year of treatment. We have examined both the attachment style of the patient to early caregivers, and the attachment between patient and therapist in the treatment itself.

Koenigsberg, H.W., Kernberg, O.F., Stone, M.H., Appelbaum, A.H., Yeomans, F.E., & Diamond, D. (2000). *Borderline patients: Extending the limits of treatability*. New York: Basic Books.

This volume by the research group at the Personality Disorders Institute takes up special problems that the therapist often encounters in treating borderline patients. These include diagnosis, sadomasochism, narcissism and psychopathy, trauma, attachment styles, schizoid states and paranoid regression, depression and suicidality, erotic transferences, medication, and understanding how TFP may be used in sequence with other therapies.

Part X: Practical Questions

Clarkin, J.C., Foelsch, P.A., Levy, K.N., Delaney, J.C., & Kernberg, O.K. (2001). The development of a psychodynamic treatment for borderline personality: A Preliminary study of behavioral change. *Journal of Personality Disorders*, 15, 487–495.

This article provides a full description of the currently-completed research on TFP that was summarized in this part of the *Primer*. A larger study with randomization of subjects into three different treatments for borderline patients is now underway.

Bateman, A., Fonagy, P. (1999). The effectiveness of partial hospitalization in the treatment of borderline personality disorder: A Randomized controlled trial. *American Journal of Psychiatry*, 156, 1563–1569, and

Bateman, A., Fonagy, P. (2001). Treatment of borderline personality disorder with psychoanalytically oriented partial hospitalization: An 18-month follow-up. *American Journal of Psychiatry*, 158, 36–42.

Although these two articles do not report on research involving TFP, they break new ground in providing evidence by means of a randomized controlled trial of the effectiveness of a psychoanalytically based treatment for borderline personality. An interesting finding was that, when studied at the follow-up point, patients receiving the psychoanalytically based treatment, in contrast to the control group, both maintained the progress they had made during their time in the study and continued to show improvement during the next 18 months.

INDEX

BIO SKETCHES

Frank E. Yeomans, M.D., Ph.D.

Frank E. Yeomans, M.D., Ph.D. is Clinical Associate Professor of Psychiatry at the Joan and Sanford I. Weill Medical College of Cornell University and Co-Director of Training and Senior Supervisor at the Personality Disorders Institute at the New York Presbyterian Hospital, Westchester Division. In addition to private practice in New York City and White Plains, NY, Dr. Yeomans teaches and supervises Transference-Focused Psychotherapy in Quebec, the Netherlands, Switzerland and Germany. In the past, Dr. Yeomans served as Unit Chief of the Long Term Borderline Unit at the New York Hospital, Westchester Division (1989–1995). He has been involved in research on the psychotherapy of borderline patients since 1985 and has authored and co-authored numerous articles. His previous books are: *Treating the Borderline Patient: A Contract-based Approach*, Basic Books, New York, 1992 (with Michael Selzer and John Clarkin); *Psychotherapy for Borderline Personality*, J. Wiley and Sons, New York, 1999 (with John Clarkin, first author, and Otto Kernberg); and *Borderline Patients: Extending the Limits of Treatability*, Basic Books, New York, 2000 (with Harold Koenigsberg, first author, Otto Kernberg, Michael Stone, Ann Appelbaum and Diana Diamond). He has also written studies on Flaubert.

John F. Clarkin, Ph.D.

Dr. Clarkin is a Professor of Clinical Psychology, Department of Psychiatry, Joan and Sanford I. Weill Medical College of Cornell University and the Co-director of the Personality Disorders Institute and the Director of Psychology at Cornell Medical Center. Dr. Clarkin is on the Research Faculty and is a Lecturer at Columbia University's Psychoanalytic Center. His research publications are on the phenomenology of personality disorders, especially borderline personality disorder. For the last 12 years, he has directed a large scale clinical study of the effect of psychodynamic psychotherapy with severely disturbed borderline personality disorder patients. He has obtained grants from the National Institute of Mental Health and the Borderline Personality Disorders Research Foundation to further this work. He is also on the editorial board of journals such as the *Journal of Personality Disorders, Clinical Psychology Review,* and the *Bulletin of the Menninger Foundation.* Known nationally and internationally for his expertise in the empirical investigation of psychotherapy, he has served on the treatment assessment committee of the NIMH, and has served as the Executive Officer of the International Society for Psychotherapy Research. He is an author of nine books and has edited four others.

Otto F. Kernberg, M.D.

Otto F. Kernberg, M.D., F.A.P.A., is Director of the Personality Disorders Institute at The New York Presbyterian Hospital, Westchester Division and Professor of Psychiatry at the Weill Medical College of Cornell University. Dr. Kernberg is Past-President of the International Psychoanalytic Association and also Training and Supervising Analyst of the Columbia University Center for Psychoanalytic Training and Research. In the past, Dr. Kernberg served as Director of the C.F. Menninger Memorial Hospital, Supervising and Training Analyst of the Topeka Institute for Psychoanalysis, and Director of the Psychotherapy Research Project of the Menninger Foundation. Later, he was Director of the General Clinical Service of the New York State Psychiatric Institute, and Professor of Clinical Psychiatry at the College of Physicians and Surgeons of Columbia University. From 1976 to 1995 he was

Associate Chairman and Medical Director of The New York Hospital-Cornell Medical Center, Westchester Division. He was awarded the 1972 Heinz Hartmann Award of the New York Psychoanalytic Institute and Society, the 1975 Edward A. Strecker Award from the Institute of Pennsylvania Hospital, the 1981 George E. Daniels Merit Award of the Association for Psychoanalytic Medicine, the 1982 William F. Schonfeld Memorial Award of the American Society for Adolescent Psychiatry, the 1986 Van Gieson Award from the New York State Psychiatric Institute, and the 1990 Mary S. Sigourney Award for Psychoanalysis. He was elected to membership of the Society of Scholars of the Johns Hopkins University in 1992. He received the 1993 I. Arthur Marshall Distinguished Alumnus Award, Menninger Alumni Association, The Menninger Foundation, the 1993 Presidential Award for Leadership in Psychiatry from the National Association of Psychiatric Health Systems, and the Distinguished Service Award from the American Psychiatric Association in 1995. He was elected Doctor Honoris Causa by the University of Buenos Aires, Argentina, in 1998, and received the Austrian Cross of Honor for Science and Art, in 1999. He is the author of 8 books and co-author of 8 others. His most recent book *Die Liebe, der Hass und die Objektbeziehung,* will be published by Psychosozial Verlag, 2001. (In press).